The Siege of
Fort Beauséjour, 1755

THE NEW BRUNSWICK MILITARY HERITAGE SERIES

1. *Saint John Fortifications, 1630 – 1956*, Roger Sarty and Doug Knight
2. *Hope Restored: The American Revolution and the Founding of New Brunswick*, Robert L. Dallison
3. *The Siege of Fort Beauséjour, 1755,* Chris M. Hand

The Siege of Fort Beauséjour
1755

CHRIS M. HAND

The New Brunswick Military Heritage Series
Volume 3

GOOSE LANE EDITIONS
and
THE NEW BRUNSWICK MILITARY HERITAGE PROJECT

Copyright © Chris M. Hand, 2004.

All rights reserved. No part of this work may be reproduced or used in any form or by any means, electronic or mechanical, including photocopying, recording, or any retrieval system, without the prior written permission of the publisher or a licence from the Canadian Copyright Licensing Agency (Access Copyright). To contact Access Copyright, visit www.accesscopyright.ca or call 1-800-893-5777.

Edited by Marc Milner.
Cover and interior design by Paul Vienneau and Julie Scriver.
NBMHP cartographer: Mike Bechthold.
Printed in Canada by Transcontinental.
10 9 8 7 6 5 4 3 2 1

Photos and other illustrative material on pages 23, 65, and 88 appear courtesy of the National Archives of Canada (NAC); on page 30, courtesy of the Canadian War Museum (CWM); on pages 10, 44, 70, 77, 84, and 96, courtesy of Parks Canada (PC); on pages 29 and 49, courtesy of the British Library (BL); on page 40, courtesy of the William L. Clements Library, University of Michigan (UM); on pages 33 and 59, courtesy of Lewis Parker (LP); and on page 29, courtesy of the New Brunswick Museum (NBM). The map on page 81 is by David Fraser, with data, courtesy of Service New Brunswick (DF, SNB). Cover illustrations: detail of photo of Fort Beauséjour (PC); interpreter wearing Compagnie franches de la Marine uniform (PC); detail of *British Soldiers at Fort Cumberland (formerly Beauséjour), 1757*, by Lewis Parker (LP).

NATIONAL LIBRARY OF CANADA CATALOGUING IN PUBLICATION DATA

Hand, Chris M., 1961-
    The siege of Fort Beausejour, 1755 / Chris M. Hand.

(New Brunswick military heritage series; 3)
Co-published by the New Brunswick Military Heritage Project.
Includes bibliographical references and index.
ISBN 0-86492-377-5

    1. Fort Beauséjour (N.B.) — Siege, 1755.   2. Acadians — Expulsion, 1755.
    I. New Brunswick Military Heritage Project.   II. Title.   III. Series.

FC384.H36 2004   971.01'8   C2004-901481-1

Published with the financial support of the Canada Council for the Arts, the Government of Canada through the Book Publishing Industry Development Program, the New Brunswick Culture and Sports Secretariat, the Canadian War Museum, and the Military and Strategic Studies Program at the University of New Brunswick.

GOOSE LANE EDITIONS	NEW BRUNSWICK MILITARY HERITAGE PROJECT
469 King Street	Military and Strategic Studies Program
Fredericton, New Brunswick	Department of History, University of New Brunswick
CANADA E3B 1E5	PO Box 4400
www.gooselane.com	Fredericton, New Brunswick
	CANADA E3C 1M4
	www.unb.ca/nbmhp

*To the late John Clarence Webster, whose efforts
secured Fort Beauséjour for future generations and
whose passion for the story still inspires.*

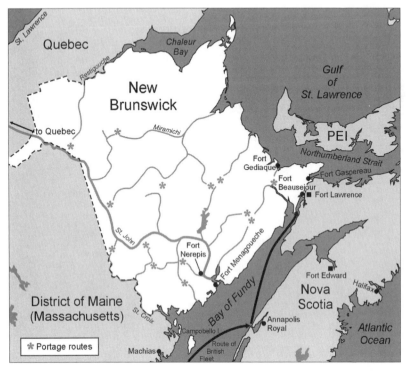

Map of New Brunswick and region, showing the locations of key places and the strategic situation in 1755.

TABLE OF CONTENTS

ACKNOWLEDGEMENTS　　9

CHAPTER ONE　　11
The Building of Fort Beauséjour
   Early Conflict in Nova Scotia, 1604-1749 12
   Fortifying the Isthmus 16

CHAPTER TWO　　31
Assembling the British Expedition

CHAPTER THREE　　45
The British Assault Begins
June 2-8, 1755
     The British Army Advances 57
     The Battle for Pont à Buot, June 4, 1755 61
     Establishment of the British Siege Camp 65
     Consolidation of the British Camp 68

CHAPTER FOUR　　71
The Siege
June 8-16, 1755
     The First Battle of Butte à Charles 72
     The Days of Waiting and Preparation 75
     The Second Battle of Butte à Charles 78
     The Formal Siege Begins 80
     Rain Delay, June 14 83
     The Bombardment Renewed, June 15-16 85
     Despair Inside the Fort 87

CHAPTER FOUR *(continued)*
The Siege
June 8-16, 1755
    Surrender, June 16 89
    Monckton's Five Terms 91
    The Surrender of Fort Gaspereau 94

CHAPTER FIVE   *97*
Peoples and Empires in the Balance

SELECTED BIBLIOGRAPHY   *103*

INDEX   *105*

ACKNOWLEDGEMENTS

My first thanks goes to the University of New Brunswick Military and Strategic Studies Program for supporting the research and encouraging my interest in the Fort Beauséjour story. I particularly wish to thank Dr. Marc Milner for the supervision of my thesis, the encouragement that helped me complete it, and the editing of the manuscript of this book. The people of Parks Canada have been extremely helpful, especially Juliette MacLeod at Fort Beauséjour and Regan Oliver at the Atlantic Service Centre in Halifax, Nova Scotia. Heather Gillis and Sue Surgeson, of Parks Canada, also helped with illustrations, as did Janet Bishop, of the New Brunswick Museum, Sandra Powlett, of the British Library, and Maurice Basque, of the Centre d'études acadiennes de l'Université de Moncton. Lewis Parker kindly allowed me to use his wonderful paintings of the fort. Thanks to Mike Bechthold and David Fraser for the maps, and to Ron Bagnell, of Service New Brunswick, and Kevin Legere, of the Nova Scotia Geological and Cartographic Service, for providing the topographical information. Thanks also to the staff of Goose Lane Editions for their wonderful production and editing, to Bill Hamilton and Jorge Sayat of the UNB Arts Faculty computer centre, to the New Brunswick Military Heritage Project for the opportunity, and to the Canadian War Museum for their financial support. Finally, thanks to Jane, Sarah, and William for their support at home.

This book is the work of many people, but the errors and omissions remain mine alone. There is much we still do not know about those tumultuous days in 1755, and I hope this book encourages others to continue the search.

A Mi'kmaq warrior, circa 1750. Such fighters, allied with the French, caused the British much trouble in Nova Scotia from 1713 until the 1760s. The French also drew on Maliseet and Abenaki in the defence of Fort Beauséjour.
FRANCIS BLACK, PC

CHAPTER ONE

The Building of Fort Beauséjour

At two o'clock in the morning on June 2, 1755, the Marquis Louis Du Pont Duchambon de Vergor, French commandant of Fort Beauséjour, awoke to the news that a British fleet lay at anchor at the entrance to Beaubassin, now known as Cumberland Basin. According to legend, Vergor dressed quickly and went to the southern bastion, hoping to catch a glimpse of the ships. Had the day been clear, he would have been able to see well down into the Bay of Fundy. However, the bay was cloaked in a thick fog, and Vergor probably did not see the British until they were well into the basin. Lieutenant-Colonel Robert Monckton, leader of the British expedition, recorded that the French failed to notice them until they were directly below the fort.

Vergor immediately dispatched couriers to Louisbourg, Quebec, and Fort Menagoueche at the mouth of the St. John River, informing them that he was under imminent attack and asking for help. Since a native runner took about a week to reach Quebec using the Petitcodiac – St. John River – Lake Temiscouata portage route, it was unrealistic to expect help from New France. Vergor's higher headquarters at Louisbourg was closer: three days' travel if a ship stood ready at Baie Verte. Then it would take at least another week for any sort of assistance to arrive from Cape Breton. As Vergor watched Monckton land his 2,500 men later that evening, he must have asked himself if he could possibly hold out that long.

Early Conflict in Nova Scotia, 1604-1749

The 1755 British assault on Fort Beauséjour was both the final act in the long battle between Britain and France for control of Acadia and the opening act of the final struggle between the two great empires for North America itself. Since its founding in 1604, the French colony comprising what is now the Maritime Provinces of Canada had been a battleground and changed hands often. By the end of the 1600s, however, the area was decidedly French, with settlements of lowland farmers clustered around Port Royal and the Minas Basin, in present-day Nova Scotia, and the headwaters of the Bay of Fundy, in the present border region between that province and New Brunswick. These were prosperous settlements based largely on land reclaimed from the sea. Their economy was well integrated within the trading patterns of eastern North America, and their produce fed English and French colonists alike. These small and often isolated Acadian settlements were also vulnerable to attack and to the shifting tides of imperial power. Indeed, in 1713, after nearly twenty-five years of continuous war, France ceded Acadia to Britain by the Treaty of Utrecht in exchange for territories lost in Europe.

However, the French and English disagreed over what actually made up Acadia. The British claimed all of historic Acadia, which included the peninsula of Nova Scotia, the current province of New Brunswick, and parts of the current state of Maine. The French, on the other hand, conceded Nova Scotia proper but refused to concede what is now New Brunswick and northern Maine, as well as modern Prince Edward Island and Cape Breton. The French chose to limit British ownership along the Chignecto Isthmus, and they also harboured ambitions to win back the peninsula and most of the Acadian settlers, who, after 1713, became subjects of the British Crown.

The de facto frontier between the two imperial powers lay along the Chignecto Isthmus, a neck of low, fertile marshlands and parallel ridges that joins the peninsula of Nova Scotia to mainland North America. At its narrowest point, the isthmus is less than twenty kilometres wide, separating the Bay of Fundy to the south from the Northumberland Strait on the north. In addition to being a natural boundary, the isthmus was critical for French imperial transportation and communications in North America. When ice closed the St. Lawrence River in November, the frozen rivers of New Brunswick became the only connection between New France and the outside world. Without the isthmus and the river system to the west, France's greatest colony along the St. Lawrence River would be completely cut off from November to April. As the historian Will Bird observed, "Chignecto was the very key to old Acadia; her importance was recognized by all claimants, the halfway house between Quebec and Louisbourg." It was only a matter of time before one side or the other secured its claim by establishing a fort at Chignecto.

In 1721, the British governor of Nova Scotia, Paul Mascarene, suggested that "a small fort could be built on the neck, held with a garrison of 150 men." He suggested two possible locations on the Fundy side of the isthmus, either the ridge of land at the Acadian town of Beaubassin (now Fort Lawrence), one of the largest and most successful of Acadian settlements, or further west on the more prominent Beauséjour ridge. However, for various reasons, a British fort on the isthmus at this time never materialized. In the meantime, British attempts to develop their new colony of Nova Scotia were hampered by an ongoing and brutal war with the Mi'kmaq, who were incited and abetted by French imperial agents.

In 1744, during the War of Austrian Succession (called King George's War in North America), Beaubassin became the staging point for French raids against British Nova Scotia. In 1746, the French commander in the region, Chevalier Pierre La Corne conducted several expeditions against the British using French regulars, militia, and native allies. The most notorious of these was the surprise attack on the British blockhouse at Grand Pré where the garrison was slaughtered and scalped. That winter the French forces stayed at Beaubassin, and La Corne used this time to pay an official visit to the region. In his report, he recommended the Beauséjour ridge as a suitable site for a fort.

It is quite probable that the French were already using Beauséjour as a camp during the 1744 raids. Not only was the ridge ideal for defence, but it was a safe distance from the Acadian inhabitants at Beaubassin, who were extremely reluctant to harbour regular French troops in their midst. Since the British claimed Beaubassin and maintained a tenuous administrative control over the settlement, the Acadians feared British reprisals. If in fact the French periodically used the Beauséjour ridge for military camps, then it is also reasonable to assume that they would have constructed the first fortifications on the isthmus. These were most likely some sort of expedient field defences, such as fascines or pickets, and perhaps even the minor earthworks that were standard at the time for any encampment. All of these would have been temporary, and no evidence of such works survive onsite or in the written records.

The War of Austrian Succession ended with the Treaty of Aix-la-Chapelle in 1748. While the French had done well in Europe, they lost a key part of their North American empire when the governor of Massachusetts, William Shirley, captured the fortress at Louisbourg in 1745. But the French understood that leaving Louisbourg in British hands meant abandoning Quebec; Acadia and Cape Breton were essential to the viability of the French empire in North America. Louisbourg was exchanged for conquests in the Netherlands and the Indian city of Madras. The British responded by establishing a new, heavily fortified capital and naval base at Halifax in 1749. The battle for Acadia — indeed for North America — was about to intensify.

With the establishment of Halifax, the French saw their chances of reconquering Nova Scotia slipping away. Concerned about Louisbourg's increasing isolation, they sought to hinder and disrupt the British settlement of Nova Scotia as much as possible without resorting to open warfare. Consequently, the low-intensity French-sponsored Anglo-Mi'kmaq war was intensified, and the colonists in Halifax suffered constant hostility from Natives and Acadians disguised as Natives. The new governor of Nova Scotia, Edward Cornwallis, rightly believed that the Indian war was nothing more than French action against the British without a formal declaration. "The warlike preparations of the French," Cornwallis wrote, "plainly evinced their hostile designs upon the British North American colonies." To forestall Acadian support for this clandestine war, Cornwallis wrote to Acadian representatives within Nova Scotia stating that he was disturbed by the goings-on and the obvious support that the French were giving the Indians. He told them in 1749 that "certain officers and missionaries who came from Canada to Chignecto last autumn have been the cause of all our troubles during the winter." A frustrated Cornwallis informed his Acadian subjects:

> We have given you also every possible assurance of the enjoyment of your religion and free and public exercise of the Roman Catholic religion. When we arrived here, we expected that

> nothing would give you so much pleasure as the determination of His Majesty to settle this province. Certainly nothing more advantageous to you could take place. You possess the only cultivated lands in the province; they produce grain and nourish cattle sufficient for the whole colony. It is you who would have had all the advantages for a long time. In short we flattered ourselves that we would make you the happiest people in the world.

Cornwallis was convinced that Nova Scotia would continue to languish as long as the French freely conducted clandestine activities and prevented the British assimilation of Nova Scotia's Acadian inhabitants. The unsettled and ill-defended boundary between French and British Acadia was a major cause of Cornwallis's problems.

Others in Europe agreed, and, in 1749, the French and British governments attempted to settle the Acadian boundary when a joint commission met in Paris. It foundered over irreconcilable claims. The British insisted on the ancient boundaries of Acadia, while the French insisted that Acadia was only the peninsula of Nova Scotia. Later that year, the French learned that the British were preparing to settle the Chignecto area. In a preventative and ultimately escalatory move, French troops secured the west side of the Missaguash River and occupied the Beauséjour ridge.

Fortifying the Isthmus

The process of fortifying the Chignecto Isthmus is the topic of a minor historical debate. The first true forts were not erected until the early 1750s, when, almost simultaneously, the French and English built forts on the Missaguash River. Historians have argued who was the first to build. Conventional wisdom and most historians suggest that it was the British. There is, however, evidence to show that the French were first, when they erected Fort Beauséjour as part of a colony-wide initiative.

Fort Beauséjour was one of several French forts erected in North America after 1748 to consolidate and strengthen their positions and establish new outposts in areas the French claimed. Consequently, they improved old forts and built new ones at key points along New France's extensive communications and transportation network of interconnected lakes, rivers, and portages. In 1749, Louisbourg was rebuilt, Fort Niagara was established at the western end of Lake Ontario, Fort Duquesne was constructed near modern-day Pittsburgh, and in 1750, Fort Rouille (now Toronto) was built at the end of the portage system from Lake Ontario to Lake Simcoe and Georgian Bay.

Renewed French activity in Acadia started in 1748, when they rebuilt the fort at the mouth of the St. John River to secure that vital waterway, prevent the English from settling the river, and protect all French inhabitants outside of the peninsula of Nova Scotia. In 1749, they also reoccupied the old fort at Nerepis, further up the St. John River. The 1748 plan also called for French troops to occupy and fortify the isthmus at Chignecto, and this project moved along with some urgency. The new governor of Canada, Pierre-Jacques de Taffanel, Marquis de la Jonquière, reinforced his predecessor's instructions and ordered the erection of a fort at Beauséjour. As a prelude, in 1759 fortified supply depots were built on Indian Island (now Skull Island) in Shediac Bay, sometimes known as Fort Gediaque, and at the head of tide on the Shediac River. From the latter, men and supplies could move across a short portage to the Petitcodiac River and down to Chignecto.

Jonquière informed Cornwallis in a letter dated October 25, 1749, that the French would prevent any effort by the British to establish themselves at Chignecto until the Acadian boundary dispute was settled. As Jonquière explained:

With respect to the river St. John, the Marquis de la Galissonniere has done quite right in sending there a good detachment. You must be well aware that I have sent one into the settlements of Delkekondiak, Memerancoug and Chipudy [Petitcodiac, Memramcook, and Shepody, settlements on the New Brunswick side of the Chignecto Isthmus]. The officers who command at those stations have orders to maintain their position, and to prevent the formation, by you, of any establishment there, until the true limits of Acadia and New France have been regulated by the two crowns.

Cornwallis considered this a direct challenge to British claims. He wrote to Jonquière, whom he seems to have known personally, on November 1, 1749 expressing his disappointment:

I am very much surprised to find that you not only approve of the conduct of M. de la Galissonniere in reference to the river St. John, but that you yourself have sent a detachment into that province as far as [Chignecto]. It is to your letter that I am indebted for the first information of this, which causes me to hope that your detachments have not yet arrived there, and that you will give orders to prevent their arrival, as I cannot possibly imagine anything more contrary to the good faith and confidence which subsist between the two crowns, or more opposed to the law of nations.

I am quite right in maintaining that until the two crowns have agreed otherwise the whole coast of St. John and those places into which you write to me that you are sending detachments are comprised in Nova Scotia. As to the places about which there could be any difficulty you cannot be ignorant that the rule is,

> There shall be no change at all, nor shall any establishment be made there, nor shall any troops be sent there.

Cornwallis reported all of this information to his superior in England, and he used it to make another plea for permission to raise a fort of his own:

> I have likewise intelligence that may be depended on, that the French have actually raised some kind of fort at Chignecto upon the River Tintramar.
>
> Your Grace will be more and more convinced of the necessity of securing that Isthmus, by a Fortress and a strong garrison. It would have been happy for this province, if it had been done last summer.

Cornwallis was already too late. Later that same fall, La Corne, with a detachment of nearly 2,500 troops from the Compagnie franches de la Marine, occupied the Beauséjour ridge. The following spring, 1750, the French fort started to take shape, most likely with some earth embankments and a log palisade. La Corne was later assisted in his work by an engineer officer from Quebec, Le Sieur de Lery. The French notary Louis De Courville recorded this event, and the British response:

> *Le Chevalier de La Corne reçut enfin ordre de se fixer un endroit propre à bâtir un fort, et il choisit l'éminence de Beauséjour, qui donnait sur le fond de la Baie Fondy. Le Sieur de Lery, fils de celui qui était Ingénieur à Québec, fut envoyé pour le tracer et le commencer, ce qu'il fit; les Anglois de leur cote en bâtirent un à Beaubassin, qu'ils nommèrent Lawrence, et y laissèrent un Commandant, et une forte garnison.*

In the spring of 1750, Governor Cornwallis finally ordered Major Charles Lawrence, one of his senior officers, to proceed to Chignecto and secure the area with a fort — despite the fact that he knew the French were already there. He also ordered one of his naval commanders, Captain John Rous, to take his ship to the St. John River and prevent any further supplies from reaching the French outposts. On May 1, Lawrence sailed into the Cumberland Basin with 400 men, intent on securing the Beauséjour ridge. He soon discovered that the French already occupied it and were well entrenched and prepared to defend their interests west of the Missaguash River. Lawrence did not have sufficient force to contest La Corne at Beauséjour and decided to move further up the basin. He attempted to land below the village of Beaubassin, on the east side of the Missaguash. Beaubassin, the largest Acadian settlement in Chignecto, occupied much of the ridge south of the present Nova Scotia tourist information centre.

Unfortunately for Lawrence, a falling tide stranded his ships, and he was forced to watch as the French and Natives emptied the village, herded the population across the Missaguash to Beauséjour, and burned all the buildings. The Abbé Le Loutre, France's *agent provocateur* in the region, had ordered that 121 buildings, including the church, mill, tannery, and brick kiln be destroyed that afternoon. Without sufficient forces or supplies to erect his own camp, Lawrence abandoned the enterprise and returned to Halifax. The French had successfully held their position and reinforced their claim that everything west of the Missaguash was sovereign French territory. But many local Acadians paid for the victory with the loss of their homes, and the French were saddled with a major refugee problem on their side of the line.

Lawrence returned that September with a larger force and the necessary stores to erect a fort. He brought nearly 700 troops, 300 from Warburton's Regiment and another 400 from Lascelles's — both regular British units stationed in Nova Scotia. He avoided the French on the

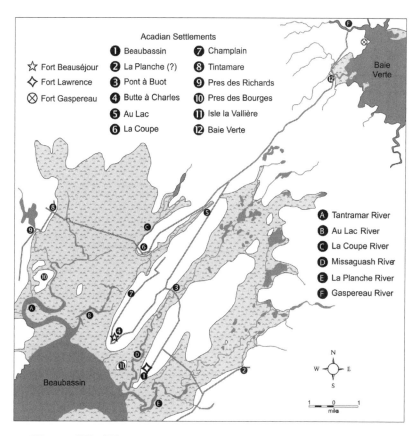

Chignecto, 1750-1755.

Beauséjour ridge and landed directly below the ruins of Beaubassin. Some Natives and some of the French disguised as Natives were there to meet him, but after a brief skirmish they withdrew. The British completed their landing, and they erected beside the ruins of the Acadian town a squared palisade, which they named Fort Lawrence. A cairn near the railway cutting now marks the site of the British fort.

Several accounts claim that the French built Fort Beauséjour in response to the British construction of Fort Lawrence in September

1750. This would appear to be only partially correct. By then the French had already entrenched on the ridge, but work on the familiar star-shaped fort, currently preserved at Beauséjour, only commenced after Fort Lawrence was completed. This may be the cause of the confusion. It is also true that Fort Beauséjour grew slowly; it was still incomplete at the time of the siege in 1755, and its defensibility was questionable. Its reputation as the third strongest French fort in North America was little more than a boast. Even though it was larger than Fort Duquesne on the Ohio, Beauséjour was considerably smaller than Fort Carillon and Fort Niagara, which both had stone-faced walls and glacis. Fort Beauséjour was completely made of earth, reinforced with timbers and palisades, and faced with multiple layers of packed sod and turf. It was only seventy-nine metres at its widest point and substantially smaller across the parade square. Despite its size, it was built along classic European lines, a pentagon with five bastions made of five-metre-high earthworks. Nonetheless, it was essentially a frontier fort, not designed to withstand a formal siege. The fort would eventually have a compliment of twenty-four cannons of various calibres, ranging from three- to twelve-pounders, although not all of them were serviceable and several were purported to have burst when fired.

None of the four commandants showed much interest in making any improvements. Upon assuming command in 1754, Vergor, the last commandant, wrote this description of his new charge:

> The fort of Beauséjour is a fairly regular pentagon, the bastions of which are rather slow in finishing, the necessary labour being short owing to lack of food. The trenches have been begun in some places, but the curtains are extremely weak. The parade is much too small. The building that serves as government stores is ready to fall to pieces and should be rebuilt. The guardhouse,

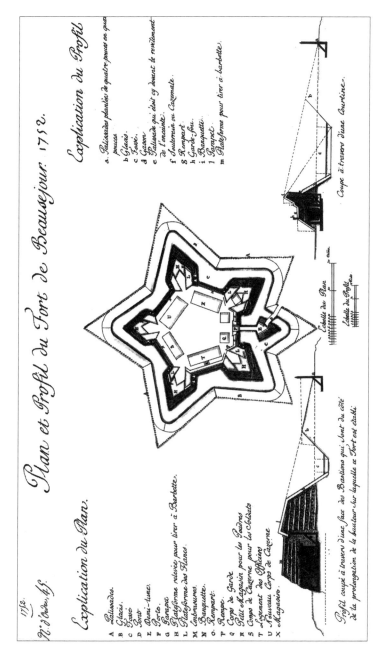

Plan and profile of Fort Beauséjour, 1752. NAC

which is on the left of the parade as you enter, is in very bad condition. There is a small house roofed with bark on the right, which serves as an office for the clerks.

All the quarters, of officers and soldiers alike, are poorly built, in bad condition, very damp, and the rain comes in everywhere. The chimneys are no more than clay, plastered on scraps of wood, and are easily washed down by the too-frequent rains. There is always danger of fire, which is the more serious in that there would be neither remedy nor escape.

The main section of the new barracks, which is not yet finished, has only two fronts. It serves at present as quarters for the Commandant and officers.

The powder magazine is very badly placed, near the gate, and is in no way protected against bombs. Another has been built which they say is fairly good.

The wells are of no use. The water is thick and muddy, and can never be made pure. They are obliged to go ten or twelve arpents [roughly 600 m] from the fort for water.

The level of the parade is a couple of feet higher than that of the buildings, which causes the dampness and leaves the mud wet.

Finally, the fort is dominated by an eminence rising directly opposite the gate. It should be changed.

There are twenty-one cannon of different calibre in the fort, one mortar, ball and other things. There may be 160 men in the fort.

The hospital is about two arpents [117m] away, and has only seven beds.

The bakery, which has two ovens recently remade, is a wretched building, and almost as far away. The labourers and employees are lodged outside the fort.

Apart from the corruption of its commandants, who stole much of the money assigned to construction, Beauséjour was also poorly sited. It was too distant from the basin to threaten shipping and too far forward on the slope to defend the crest. The French simply could not afford to build a fort large enough to do both, and the crest (Butte à Charles) was already occupied by an Acadian village. Given the shape of the ridge at that point, it would have been difficult to make the fort much bigger without pushing the walls down the slope or flattening the crown of the ridge. Both of these options would have required enormous labour. A profile of the fort and ridge shows the fort about 400 metres south of the crest. The British used this flaw to their advantage during the siege and subsequently corrected the problem by erecting outer works (which still exist) at the crest. Overall, Fort Beauséjour never realized its full potential under the French. Nor, apart from a small redoubt at Pont à Buot (now corrupted to Point de Bute), did the French attempt to fortify the approaches to Fort Beauséjour by siting advanced batteries on key features along the Missaguash River. Arguments continue as to whether or not a determined and dedicated garrison could have made a difference.

Inadequate as it was, Fort Beauséjour was the centrepiece of the French defences on the isthmus and central to two satellite forts. The first was Fort Menagoueche at the mouth of the St. John River. It was a simple square palisade, with an outer work covering the gate and a few guns to control entrance to the river. It guarded the entrance to the main interior route to New France, and it was linked to Chignecto by the Bay of Fundy and river and portage routes along the Kennebecasis and Petitcodiac rivers. No trace of Fort Menagoueche survives, and its original site is now under the toll booth for the Harbour Bridge.

The second satellite fort was built the same year as Fort Beauséjour on the north side of the isthmus at Baie Verte, near the mouth of the Gaspereau River. Fort Gaspereau secured the northern side of the isthmus

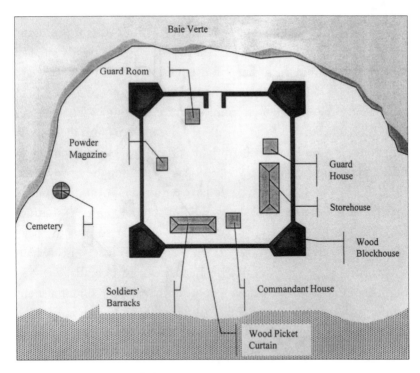

Plan of Fort Gaspereau, 1755.

and replaced the depots at Shediac, which were abandoned. Vergor described it as follows:

> This stronghold was named Fort Gaspereau, after the river there. The fort was in the form of a square and the four bastions were solidly constructed of huge timbers. On the platforms were mounted six cannon. The curtains consisted of two rows of pickets, driven against each other, behind, which was a bank of earth four feet wide and nearly four feet in height. A fosse was excavated six feet from the enclosure. The garrison was small, consisting of an officer and fifteen regulars.

When John Winslow, a lieutenant-colonel of the colonial troops from Massachusetts, took over Fort Gaspereau in June 1755, he was unimpressed with the structure, which was in a horrendous state of repair.

> [We] took possession of the garrison which I take to be one hundred and eighty foot square with four bad blockhouses, one at each corner, a ditch partly dug, no ramparts, not glacis, nor an estrodenary palisade, a large storehouse but not tight nor floor. Neither is there a building in the whole tenantable, all things are miserable to the last degree.

Fort Gaspereau was never intended for serious defence; instead, it was a protected warehouse and shipping station for supplies from Louisbourg and Quebec. In this capacity it served well and was the main point of entry for most goods brought into the isthmus and most Acadian exports to French colonies. a rough road linked it to Beauséjour by 1752. The original trace of Fort Gaspereau is well preserved just outside Port Elgin.

Thus, by the spring of 1751 the Chignecto Isthmus had developed into an armed frontier with three forts, two French and one British, and close to a thousand armed soldiers lived and patrolled along its length. At the southern end, along the banks of the Missaguash River, Fort Beauséjour and the British Fort Lawrence were only three kilometres apart and in plain view of each other. In fact, the situation on the Chignecto Isthmus was without parallel in the whole of North America. It was the only place where French and British forces were close enough to see each other and have direct contact.

This proximity led to all sorts of unique arrangements. British soldiers traded with Acadians and their Native allies by day and were attacked by them at night. Commanders on both sides corresponded regularly and made local agreements to exchange wandering livestock and even deserters. Sometimes goods were reluctantly exchanged between the two, and local Acadians often sought employment for British gold instead of French silver. All the while, French provocateurs and priests worked hard, by persuasion and by the threat of violence, to keep the Acadian population of British Nova Scotia loyal to the French crown and Catholicism. In turn, the British worked equally hard to stop this.

Meanwhile the Anglo-Mi'kmaq war continued. In February 1751, Cornwallis tried once again to gather support from Massachusetts to settle the Acadian and Indian problems in Nova Scotia. The most powerful and moving argument was invoking the fear of a French invasion of the colony:

> For if the French should make a strong settlement on the South Coast in these parts and thereby gain a nearer communications with the Indians on our frontiers and have the opportunity of supplying them with warlike stores and other things the probability in that case of the whole province of main as well as the lands between that and the river of St. Croix being swallowed up by the French is obvious to every considerate person.

Cornwallis's words were prophetic. This is exactly what the French were doing, and Fort Beauséjour was their starting point. From their garrison at the north end of the Bay of Fundy they were able to resupply and encourage their Native allies in Nova Scotia. For the moment, however, Cornwallis had little luck in convincing his masters in England that the threat presented to New England and Nova Scotia was worth the price of war. And so the Chignecto Isthmus remained an armed camp, with the French and the British warily watching each other across the Missaguash River while the war inside Nova Scotia continued. This situation could not last. The next three years were marked by increasing hostility, distrust, and a growing determination by the British to solve the problem once and for all.

Fort Lawrence at the time of the siege of Fort Beauséjour. By 1755, the considerable settlement that had developed south of the fort was tied into it with high palisades, the sign of a community under siege. A cairn beside the railway on the road south of the Nova Scotia Tourist Bureau now marks the site of the fort. NBM, BL

A soldier of Les Compagnies franches de la Marine, the unit which built and manned the fort, in summer campaign dress for North America. He has discarded his long grey-white surcoat (shown on the cover) for the season, using his navy blue long-sleeved waistcoat as an outer garment. Moccasins and buckskin leggings replace boots, a hatchet has replaced his short sword and a soft fatigue cap is worn in place of the tricorne hat. R. MARRION, CWM

CHAPTER TWO

Assembling the British Expedition

"The almost continual war we have with the Indians prevents our mixing any English settlers with these Inhabitants [Acadians] or instituting any sort of civil jurisdiction among them," Peregrine Thomas Hopson, the new governor of Nova Scotia explained to London in 1752. Acadians, he observed, "have been hitherto left open to the insinuations and evil practices of French priests and emissaries that are set amongst them from Canada and the French Fort at Beauséjour." Moreover, not only were the French fomenting trouble among the Acadians — who were, after all, British subjects — and waging an undeclared war in Nova Scotia, but their new forts at Beauséjour, Gaspereau and the mouth of the St. John River were in fact on British soil. For Hopson, as for his predecessor, Cornwallis, Beauséjour was the nub of the problem.

> They have a strong fort at Beauséjour and are every day adding new works to it; of this, indeed, I can speak with some certainty as their fort is in sight of ours. . . . On their festivals upwards of 300 have been seen about their Mass House . . . they all have arms and ammunition and orders to repair to the fort upon any alarm.

Something had to be done about the fort on the west side of the Missaguash.

The British were correct in their assessment of French intentions, and the Acadians, anxious to be left alone to farm, were victimized by a French campaign of terror. Those who refused to move to the west of the Missaguash were attacked by Natives and denied the ministry of priests. The architect of this campaign and the undeclared war in Nova Scotia was Abbé Jean-Louis Le Loutre, Vicar to the Mi'kmaq. Le Loutre is perhaps the most villainous character in the whole Beauséjour story. All of the British and most of the French accounts paint Le Loutre in a bad light. He first came to Nova Scotia in 1737, with British permission, as a missionary to minister to the Acadians and Natives at Shubenacadie under the terms of the Treaty of Utrecht. In exchange, Le Loutre promised to keep the peace and to keep the people faithful to the British crown. Instead, he proved a loyal and zealous advocate for France, encouraging the Mi'kmaq to attack English settlers and offering one hundred livres bounty for each English scalp.

During the War of Austrian Succession, Le Loutre moved to Beaubassin as the newly appointed Vicar General of Acadia, where his hostility to the British was unmasked. When the British landed at Beaubassin in 1750, it was Le Loutre who ordered the town burned and the residents driven to the French side of the Missaguash River. He then took up residence at Fort Beauséjour, where the commandants supported his activities. Cornwallis issued orders for his arrest, but Le

Lewis Parker's modern painting of the interior of the fort, circa 1754. The large two-storey building is the "new" barracks; it stood in front of what is now the stone curtain wall on the southeastern side of the fort. In the centre, Abbé Le Loutre, France's agent provocateur in the Anglo-Mi'kmaq war, talks to a senior officer. LP

Loutre remained free to intimidate the Acadians and abet Native attacks on Nova Scotia.

Nothing had been resolved by the time Charles Lawrence, who had originally built Fort Lawrence, succeeded Hopson as governor of Nova Scotia in 1753, so Lawrence took steps to curtail French activities in his province. He wanted to stop the flow of aid to the Mi'kmaq, end the "illegal" trade between Acadian and British settlers that supplied both Beauséjour and Louisbourg, and force the Acadians to take an oath of loyalty. As a result, in 1754, the commandant of Fort Lawrence was ordered to prevent anyone from supplying the French garrison at Beauséjour with provisions.

I am ordered to acquaint you that if Mr. Arbuckle [a Boston trader] or any other person should offer to supply the French Garrison at Beauséjour with provisions, that you are directed to take all measures to prevent it, as we all know that the French buy up such provision for the use of the Indians in order to encourage them to make war upon His Majesty's subjects in this province.

Louisbourg, in particular, was dependent upon New England grain, which Lawrence was able to block, with severe consequences for the French garrison in the region. On September 17, 1754, he issued a proclamation forbidding the exportation of corn from the province, explaining, "The two principal and important reasons for passing this law were, firstly, to prevent the supplying of corn to the Indians and their abettors, who residing on the north side of the Bay of Fundy do commit hostilities upon His Majesty's subjects, which they cannot so conveniently do, that supply being cut off, and secondly, for the better supplying of the Halifax market."

Lawrence's embargo had an almost immediate effect. It became exceedingly difficult for the French to support not only their garrisons, but also the Acadian refugees from Beaubassin who had crowded into the settlements west of the Missaguash. Several letters allude to their plight, and French officials complained that they could not secure enough provisions to assist these people. Consequently, Acadian refugees longed to return to their fertile farms on the British side of the Missaguash, despite various new projects to create more farmland on the French side. Caught between the two warring empires, some Acadians succumbed to British pressure, returned to Nova Scotia, took the oath, and settled back on their old lands. But most did not. As Lawrence explained to London on August 1, 1754:

> I believe that they [the Acadians] have at present laid aside all thoughts of taking the Oaths voluntarily, and great numbers of them are at present gone to Beauséjour to work for the French.
>
> They have not for a long time brought anything to our markets, but on the other hand have carried everything to the French and Indians, whom they have always assisted with provisions, quarters, and intelligence, and indeed while they remain without taking the Oaths to his majesty — which they will never do till they are forced.
>
> As they possess the best and largest tracts of land in this province, it cannot be settled with any effect while they remain in this situation.

What prompted the British to finally take military action was the discovery in late 1754 that France intended to reinforce its North American garrisons and intensify the frontier war. In particular, the British intercepted a letter from the governor in Quebec to Le Loutre, dated November 9, 1754, that outlined these plans. The message invited Le Loutre and the commandant of Fort Beauséjour, Vergor, to continue their attacks. The governor wrote:

> The present position of Canada demands that those natives which are strongly connected should strike without delay; provided the order shall not appear to come from me, because I have precise instructions to remain on the defensive. This I leave you to manage every thing for the peace, which I look upon as a feint for your savages — in this scheme of the English, they wish to confine us in such a manner as to prevent our leaving without being seen by them. This increases the necessity of striking with energy, for you know better than I that ten scalps

would stop an English army — a very lucky circumstance, because by their large numbers they would soon overrun this country.

By 1754, the French were also raiding into Massachusetts, New Hampshire, and New York.

The day that Lawrence received a copy of this letter, two more British soldiers were found scalped near Fort Lawrence. He needed nothing else to convince him of the need for action. Writing to London, Lawrence recommended that a "body of men in New England which joined to a few troops we could muster be sent to demolish Fort Beauséjour, and when that is done the French Inhabitants on that side must either be removed to this, or driven totally away by fire and sword."

Even before they received Lawrence's appeal, British authorities had resolved to settle the French problem in North America. In early January 1755, the British mobilized naval and military forces to meet the threat of a French offensive along the colonial frontier. On April 10, Vice-Admiral Edward Boscawen was ordered to sail for North America, interdict the French fleet sailing for Quebec, blockade Louisbourg, and fall upon any French ships attempting to land troops in Nova Scotia or to go to Cape Breton or to pass through the St. Lawrence to Quebec.

On land, a three-pronged assault on French possessions was planned. General Edward Braddock was sent to America with two regiments to lead the main attack in the Ohio basin at Fort Duquesne. A second thrust would move up the Hudson River – Lake Champlain valley. The third attack would strike the French forts in Acadia, using local forces raised by the governors of Nova Scotia and Massachusetts. On November 5, 1754, Lawrence wrote to Governor Shirley, proposing that they attack before the French did. If they moved early enough, Lawrence believed, the French would be unable to assemble a large force at Beauséjour because the restrictions imposed by the British blockade made it impossible for them to sustain large numbers of troops at Chignecto. To ensure that the French were isolated at Beauséjour, Lawrence had also dispatched two ships to patrol the bay. The time to strike was now.

Shirley did not need persuading. He had already briefly outlined his concept of operations in a letter to London:

> It is universally agreed by every English officer of Nova Scotia, with whom I have conversed here, as a thing certain that the principal French fort at Beauséjour may be easily cut off from their water, which it is said they are obliged to fetch at half a mile's distance from the Fort, as they might likewise from supplies and provisions or store, all which they must receive from Louisbourg, either through Bay Verte or the Bay of Fundy, so that in case it should prove difficult to reduce them by force of artillery, yet it seems very practical to starve the garrison into surrender, provided we have a sea force superior or equal to that of the French in those two Bays to prevent their being supported from Louisbourg with recruits or provisions.

He added that he was coordinating the expedition with Lawrence and finalizing a reasonable schedule:

> We shall be able to agree upon measures in a very few weeks for the reduction of the French forts early in next year in case it should be his Majesty's pleasure to have that done. These orders should arrive here by the latter end of March or the first week in April to be in time for beginning the operations early in the year.

To coordinate plans, Lawrence sent one of his senior colonels, Robert Monckton, to Boston. With Shirley's support and enough men, Lawrence believed that they could take to the field as early as March 1755. Towards this end, Lawrence gave Monckton a letter of credit with two of the most prominent Boston merchants, Apthorp and Hancock, to purchase the necessary stores. These included twelve cannon and their "appurtenances," as well as 100 rounds of ammunition and 150 barrels of powder; harnesses were to be acquired for fifty horses, and 500 picks, 500 iron-shod shovels, and fifty wheel barrows. Tents, small arms, flints, uniforms, and "other things necessary for the troops" were all to be secured in Boston, or New York if necessary. Monckton's instructions from Lawrence also included a scheme of campaign:

> But, if it should so happen that you do not hear from me before the beginning of March, you are in that case, as soon as you think the weather will permit you to take the field, to hire sufficient number of vessels to transport your troops, artillery, baggage and warlike stores, and to proceed to Chignecto, and there to use your endeavours to take the French fort at Beauséjour, as that is the principle place they have.
>
> You are then to send a detachment such as you shall deem sufficient to summon to surrender a small fort the French have built at a Place called Gaspereau on or near the Bay of Verte.

On February 29, 1755, Governor Lawrence sent additional instructions to Monckton:

> On your arrival at Chignecto, you are to take upon you the command of the troops in garrison there as well as those of the expedition, and if you think proper, to exchange or draw out any part of them you shall want to take with you, observing always to a sufficient number of troops to defend the fort.
>
> You are to signify to the French inhabitants in the King's name,

by proclamation or the most public method you can devise, that such as do not bring in their arms to you are thereby declared rebels and may expect to be treated accordingly, and in such manner you are to proceed with them.

When you have the Fort of Beauséjour in possession, you must cause the breach or other damage received by your canon to be repaired and to garrison it securely with regular troops before you proceed to St. John's River.

After having performed the service mentioned in your former instructions, you are to proceed to the St. John's River, and do your utmost to dislodge the French from any forts or settlements they have made there within your reach and to burn and destroy such forts and settlements, behaving to any French garrisons you may find there, as directed in your former instructions, concerning the French garrisons on the isthmus. But you are on no account to undertake this service until you are in possession of the French Fort at Beauséjour and have erased every fort or post they may have establish on the isthmus of Chignecto.

When all the service herein mentioned is performed you are to come to Mines [Minas] and Pisiquid and there await orders.

If any New England Irregulars should show desire to sit down on the deserted lands at Chignecto and establish a settlement there, you will give them all due encouragement.

Monckton was kept busy throughout the winter of 1754-1755, finalizing the preparations and recruiting the necessary colonial troops for the expedition. Shirley believed that a thousand New Englanders would be a "sufficient force to secure the success of that service and drive the French of Canada out of the province." To raise them, Shirley needed a native New Englander who was experienced, well known throughout

Robert Monckton as a brigadier at the time of the siege of Quebec, 1759. UM

the colony, and trusted and respected by the population. He selected Marshfield-born John Winslow.

"Winslow," wrote Shirley, "hath the best reputation as a military man of any officer in this province [Massachusetts] and his character in every respect stands high with the Government and people and he is particularly well esteem'd and belov'd by the soldiery." At fifty-two, Winslow was old for such an expedition. But he was an experienced soldier, having campaigned in Nova Scotia recently and earned a substantive rank in the regular British army. In 1754, as major-general of militia, he led an 800-man expedition to the Kennebec River in Maine, where he built forts to secure the area. Therefore, in the spring of 1755, it was natural for Shirley to select Winslow to lead the New England component of the Beauséjour expedition. He was to "take command of the two battalions of the regiment and order them to place of rendezvous on April 10, supply them with clothing and such arms as can be produced in Boston, embark them with their arms, ammunition and provisions, and sail with them as soon as the weather permits to Nova Scotia, where they shall be landed at such a place as Monckton directs." Winslow was ordered to recruit men "able-bodied, free from body ailments and of perfect limbs," but no Roman Catholics nor any man under five foot four inches. It was not hard to find volunteers. New Englanders had fought the French along their frontier for as long as anyone could remember, and the upcoming war took on the proportions of a religious crusade that tapped into the strong vein of anti-Catholicism deep in the Puritan roots of Massachusetts and New England. Winslow had a fairly easy time raising nearly 2,000 volunteers. The men were mustered in Boston in early April and divided into nineteen companies, in two battalions. One was commanded by Lieutenant-Colonel Winslow himself, the other placed under Lieutenant-Colonel George Scott, a regular officer from Monckton's regiment.

Command of the naval part of the expedition fell to another native New Englander, John Rous. One of the most interesting characters of the era, Rous made a name for himself in the 1740s as a privateer, cruising the Grand Banks, raiding the fishing fleets, capturing a small French fleet, and destroying fishing stations and fishing boats. He was second in command of New England vessels at Louisbourg in 1745, and was rewarded by a commission as a captain on the active list in the Royal Navy on September 24, 1745. In the years of peace that followed, Rous patrolled in the Bay of Fundy as part of the British attempt to exert sovereignty over the area and check the flow of supplies to the clandestine war in Nova Scotia. On one occasion, he captured a brig and several prisoners, among them the future commandant of Fort Beauséjour, Vergor. Rous was a superb naval officer and already familiar with the treacherous waters of Fundy. He was an ideal choice for the naval command, which included three twenty-gun frigates — Rous's new ship, the *Mermaid*, the *Success*, and the *Sereh* — and some forty transports. After a false start, the expedition, with the men of Shirley's Regiment embarked, finally left Boston on May 19, 1755.

About the same time, Lawrence issued his final ultimatum to the Acadians to declare their loyalty to the British Crown. His warning was clear: Captain Murray at Fort Lawrence was to advise them that their "happiness and future welfare depends very much on their present behaviour and that they may be assured if any inhabitant either old or young should offer to go to Beauséjour, or take up arms, or induce others to commit any act of hostility upon the English, or make any declaration in favour of the French, they will be treated as rebels."

The fleet hugged the coast of Maine and sailed by Grand Manan Island on the night of May 25, before crossing the mouth of the Bay of Fundy towards Nova Scotia the next day. That evening, the squadron sailed into the Annapolis Basin, leaving the three frigates anchored at the entrance to the basin (near the current ferry dock at Digby). There the final elements of Monckton's force were assembled. These included regular British soldiers from the 40th and 45th regiments of foot, drawn from garrisons throughout Nova Scotia, and a detachment of artillery and gunners from Halifax. On May 31, the squadron sailed for Chignecto under continual rain, arriving at the entrance to the Cumberland Basin in the evening of June 1. The fleet had made a remarkably rapid passage up the Bay of Fundy and now lay in wait for the tide to carry them the final treacherous nine miles through the silt-laden waters of the basin. The planning and preparations were over. The British assault on Fort Beauséjour was about to begin.

An Acadian militiaman, mid-eighteenth century. Like most North American frontier militiamen, he is distinguished from an ordinary civilian only perhaps by his bedroll, buckskin leggings, and musket. DEREK FITZJAMES, PC

CHAPTER THREE

The British Assault Begins
June 2-8, 1755

One of the great tragedies for the French in Acadia, and indeed in North America, was that their fate rested in the hands of the Marquis Louis Du Pont Duchambon de Vergor. The son of Louis Du Pont Duchambon, the commander of Louisbourg who surrendered the fortress to New Englanders in 1745 after a forty-day siege, Vergor was not much of a soldier. Born into a military family in 1712 at Placentia, Newfoundland, he joined the Compagnie franche de la Marine in 1737 and served without distinction throughout New France. Title and influence nonetheless assured him of promotion, eventually to the command of Fort Beauséjour on August 18, 1754. His mentor, the corpulent François Bigot, Intendant of New France, told him, "Profit, my dear Vergor, by your opportunity [at Beauséjour]; trim, cut — you have the power — in order that you may very soon join me in France and purchase an estate near me." Considered grasping, ill-natured, and deceitful, Vergor took Bigot's advice. By June 1755, after a year of mounting tension along the Chignecto frontier, he had done nothing to strengthen the fort, and his failure to accept advice from some of his more competent officers to forestall the British advance revealed him to be totally unfit for command.

On the afternoon of June 2, 1755, while Vergor scrambled about the ramparts of his fort, Monckton held a council of war aboard his flagship, the *Success*, at the entrance to Cumberland Basin. At the table were Colonels Monckton, Winslow, and Scott, three captains of the British regulars, and four Provincial majors. The council decided to commence landing at Fort Lawrence on the evening high tide. As Monckton recorded, a small vessel returning from the upper reaches of the basin "brought word that everything was well at Fort Lawrence and that by all the intelligence Captain Hussey [the commandant] could get, the French were not expecting them." At four o'clock in the afternoon, the fleet sailed on a rising tide.

Also watching the basin that day from the ramparts of Fort Beauséjour was Jacau de Fiedmont, an impeccably honest Canadien gunner whose valour was acknowledged by friend and foe. Fiedmont left a wonderful account of the siege — the best on the French side — in which he confirmed that the British fleet arrived on the evening tide. He and his fellow French officers used a telescope to count off the British ships as they entered the basin, tallying between thirty-seven and forty vessels of all types. British lists name only thirty-four vessels and their captains, leading to the conclusion that the French likely counted anything under sail, including small tenders and dispatch ships, vessels probably not entered on the official British list. Such was the case with the sloop of war *Vulture* and three other transports, as well as Sylvanus Cobb's sloop, the *York*, that was permanently stationed at Fort Lawrence. Regardless of the actual number, it is unlikely that many of the inhabitants of Chignecto had ever seen so many ships under sail at one time, and that all of them were under the British ensign could only mean serious trouble.

On June 2, Vergor's main hope was that the British fleet would suffer catastrophe in the final approach or in disembarking — enough to delay or even cancel their plans. This was, in fact, a reasonable expectation. For example, Lawrence's original expedition to Beaubassin in 1750 had stranded at low tide. During the later siege of November 1776, when Fort Cumberland (the British name for Beauséjour) was attacked by rebels, the British relief force waited on board ships for several weeks off what is now Fundy National Park for the wind to change; they never did sail into the basin but were forced to land troops on the shore of Minas Basin and march them overland. But in 1755, the spring weather and wind were favourable, and Captain Rous brought his fleet into the basin unhindered.

By any standards, the British arrival before Beauséjour was a remarkable feat of seamanship. Even today, there is not a lot of room in the basin for over forty vessels, and 250 years ago the situation was no better. The deepest section, called Five Fathoms Hole by the locals, is slightly west of the mouth of the Tantramar River. It is the only place where anchorage is possible at low tide; the rest is a broad expanse of muddy flats or steeply sloping banks. Moreover, the tide range in this upper reach of the Bay of Fundy is about twelve metres, and the water is totally opaque with suspended silt. The tide swirls in and out at four to five knots, and muddy water makes seeing the bottom anywhere impossible. At high tide ships can approach the shoreline for a brief period, and on the rising tide it is possible to float smaller vessels up the rivers for several kilometres. Movement by sailing vessels therefore required a fine balance of sail power and use of the tidal flow. Stranding a vessel on rapidly drying mud flats was a serious hazard. In July 1751, shortly after the British built Fort Lawrence, a brigantine from Boston ran aground and foundered during a gale off Beauséjour ridge. The stranded vessel was subsequently attacked at low tide by Natives, looted, and burned, and its crew was captured. The same thing happened to a schooner in February that same year. No pleasure craft sail in the Cumberland Basin today, and only skilled mariners did so in the age of sail.

Unfortunately for Vergor, the British were very skilled mariners. John Rous also knew the basin well. In 1750, while in command of the *Albany*, he had accompanied Major (now Governor) Lawrence's expedition to Beaubassin, and in the five years since that first landing, he had made several resupply runs out of Halifax. The records indicate that he had gathered sufficient information to create rough navigation charts of the basin, and that the British used them in 1755 to good effect. There was no need, as some historians have speculated, for Rous to "sound" his way in using lead lines cast from the leading ships, nor, as one naval historian has also suggested, for lashing several ships together and "kedging" their way into the basin, crabbing forward using their anchors. Given the tremendous tidal surge in the Cumberland Basin, it is more likely that the British fleet was simply carried in by the sea, using their sails to provide power for what little steerage was necessary and dropping temporary channel markers as they went. Moreover, the presence of fog indicates a favourable southerly breeze over the chilly waters of the bay, ideal for a rapid and uneventful passage to Fort Lawrence.

On the evening of June 2, 1755, the British set about disembarking their troops and equipment below Fort Lawrence in full view of the French. Unloading groups of men and equipment into small boats and ferrying them ashore was a slow process. To make it faster, Monckton allowed three vessels to ground at low tide on the flats below Fort Lawrence, where there were sufficient troops to guard them until they were refloated. Despite this, it took almost two full days to complete the initial disembarkation, which included landing the field cannon needed

A view of Fort Beauséjour, the ridge, and the surrounding area, 1755. The buildings to the right of the fort, on Butte à Charles, including the hospital, the old church, and the new church on the ridge line, were burned by the French during the campaign to clear fields of fire. The high ground just above the title plate is Butte à Roger. BL

The British Assault Begins | 49

for the campaign to invest the fort. The heavy stores and equipment needed for the siege, especially the heavier guns and mortars, were brought ashore much later.

The French could only watch as the British landed on the east side of the Missaguash. Ships in the basin were out of range of even the biggest of Fort Beauséjour's cannons, just as the guns on the British ships could not reach the fort. Nonetheless, there were things that could be done to confound and delay the British. When Vergor called an immediate council of war on the evening of June 2, Fiedmont, his master gunner, urged an improvement to the northern ramparts, the obvious weak spot in the fort's defences, overlooked by higher ground from Butte à Charles. The commandant agreed and promised to provide as many men as possible for the work. Small detachments were also sent out to guard key points along the river and observe the British.

While the French soldiers hastily improved their defences, church bells rang out the alarm, and the summons went out to the local population to send armed and able-bodied men to the fort. The Acadians responded, as was their duty, but they did so slowly and reluctantly, with most of them not reporting until June 4. Many took the time to hide their families in the woods and bury their valuables first; this was how they had survived British raids in the past. Eventually, over three hundred men responded to the call, increasing the size of the garrison in Fort Beauséjour to around seven hundred Acadians, Natives, and colonial troops of the Compagnie franches de la Marine.

Meanwhile, across the Missaguash, the British expedition organized itself. Officers found quarters with the regulars inside the Fort Lawrence and in private houses outside. Several colonial officers, including John Winslow, were housed with a prominent citizen, Sylvanus Cobb. Most of the troops camped about the ruins of the village of Beaubassin and around the walls of the fort. The regulars set out neat and orderly camps, separate from the New Englanders, with proper latrines and garbage disposal. The Provincials' camps were, according to Monckton, "chaotic by comparison." Being wholly unused to living in large numbers and in such cramped conditions, the New England volunteers did not understand the basics of military camp life, especially the requirement for some sort of regulated regime and proper hygiene. After the siege, Monckton complained to his two Provincial battalion commanders, Winslow and Scott, that "many of [the New Englanders] have not changed their shirts since first putting them on in Boston," almost six weeks earlier. The Provincials often dumped their garbage outside their tents, built expedient latrines, and defecated where they felt the urge, which created breeding grounds for disease. Winslow issued several orders to improve the situation to prevent having the men fall sick. "It is observed," wrote Winslow, "that the soldiers are not so exact as could be wished in regard to cleanliness of the Camp, leaving their cabbage leaves, pease pods, etc., among their tents which, in little time will become noisome." Proper latrines and a collective garbage dump outside the camp perimeter almost immediately improved the situation, and Winslow commented that they began to "clear ourselves of one of the Egyptian plagues." Despite these precautions, the New Englanders suffered substantial sickness and disease towards the end of the expedition in September. Provincial soldiers were nevertheless a very eager bunch. Abijah Willard, one of the New England captains, thought that his troops looked impressive with their soldier-like bearing and their eagerness to work.

While the habits of the Provincials disgusted the British regulars and reinforced the notion that colonials were poor soldiers, for their part the Provincials were equally disturbed by the actions of the regulars. They were bothered by the British regular soldier's lack of piety and resented the obvious favouritism they received, being excused from certain tasks and most manual labour. The majority of this type of work was delegated to Provincials, in part because they were not as well trained in military tasks, but also because the Provincial volunteers were often more used to manual labour. In addition, many were craftsmen and tradesmen, whereas their British counterparts had no such skills. Artisans and tradesmen were particularly sought after by regular officers and often employed in their trade. Unskilled Provincials could haul and dig, and, in fact, the New Englanders did the lion's share of the heavy labour during the expedition. The British utilized that eagerness, as one officer commented, "to work our boats, drive our wagons, and fell our trees, and to do the works that in inhabited countries are performed by peasants." The lack of draught animals also meant that the New Englanders had to perform that duty as well.

While troops and stores were brought ashore at Fort Lawrence, the British sent out small patrols for security and reconnaissance. They set out pickets, as well as small detachments, to watch the dikes and guard against incursion, particularly by the Natives. There is no record of any raids by Natives while the British were encamped about Fort Lawrence, and the French seemed content to leave them alone. They also sent out scouting parties to remove French pickets and secure the western bank of the Missaguash River at Butte à Roger (the southern end of Mount Whatley, now removed for the four-lane highway) and on Tonge's Island, then known as Isle la Vallière. These forays were all met by the French at the river and repelled. Fiedmont remarked, "a few English crossed to our side on the pretext of recovering their cattle; they were stopped by M. de Langy, officer of the troops from Cape Breton, who was in charge of an observation post [at Butte à Roger] on our side; they had come presumably merely to examine the ground over which their troops were to pass."

While this was going on, the remainder of the British troops conducted drills and manoeuvres outside their fort in full view of the French. This accomplished two things, but the most important was to drill the men. The regulars, a composite force, needed to spend some time becoming a cohesive unit; the Provincials needed all the practice they could get. Having only received their weapons just before leaving Boston, many had probably never fired them. Contrary to modern notions of colonial frontiersmen, most of the New England recruits were semi-rural farm hands and labourers with little or no musketry skill. Only a few were frontiersmen or rangers. Winslow wanted every man to "pass a ball down his barrel at least once." This inexperience would not have instilled great British confidence in their abilities, and it is one of the reasons that the Provincials were usually employed as simple labourers. It also likely explains why Monckton planned to hold his regular soldiers in reserve for a final assault on the fort.

The second reason for the open-air drilling was to put on a show of force to intimidate the French, who could see the size of the army arrayed against them. It was quite a sight, the largest ever assembled at Chignecto. Lines and columns of uniformed men paraded with four regimental colours flying: Winslow's, Scott's, and those of the two regular regiments, the 40th and 45th of foot. If the French were worried, the Acadians must have been on the verge of panic. Seeing all this, the French redoubled their efforts to improve Fort Beauséjour. Fiedmont, acting as engineer, installed new pickets for the palisade and shored up the bastions and the glacis with new earth and fresh turf. But in reality there was not much he could have done that would have substantially improved the fort. He had neither the manpower nor the time, and the British were soon ready to march. The only hope for Vergor and his garrison was the speedy arrival of a relief expedition from Louisbourg, a faint hope at best.

Monckton held another council of war that first night in his quarters at Fort Lawrence. The council included all his senior infantry officers as well as artillerymen and engineers newly arrived from Halifax. Having been commandant at Fort Lawrence, Monckton probably had been thinking about how to take Fort Beauséjour for some time. He most likely explained those plans that evening and let the men go to complete their "battle procedure" and preparations.

Monckton's plan had three distinct phases. The first was to cross the Missaguash at the head of tide at Pont à Buot and establish a base camp on the far side near the high feature at Mount Whatley, then known as Butte à Mirande. The second phase was to consolidate his position on the French side of the river, move his heavy siege equipment into place, and isolate the fort. This would provide a secure base on the French side of the river, providing a point of assembly and departure for the final approach on Fort Beauséjour and security against the threat of a French relief force arriving from Baie Verte. Once safely established across the river, Monckton could bring supplies directly up the Missaguash with the tidal surge, using small boats to carry the heavy siege guns and mortars that could not be dragged across the marsh. Next, he would locate a suitable place for a gun line. The final phase was besieging and capturing the fort, either by bombarding it into submission or starving the French out. But first he had to cross the river. He chose Pont à Buot where the Acadians had constructed a stout timber bridge over the Missaguash at the first reasonable place to cross the marsh from one ridge to the other. Monckton knew that this bridge was the only route by which an army could move across the river and the tidal mud flats.

To guard this crucial bridge across the Missaguash River, the French had only a detachment of about eight soldiers under Ensign de Barallon manning a small redoubt. The post had been constructed several years earlier to limit contact with the British, stop the Acadians from crossing the river and trading with Fort Lawrence, and, most importantly, prevent them from returning to their old homes in Nova Scotia. In June 1755, the redoubt consisted of a triangular enclosure made by double rows of palisades, banked and sodded inside. Platforms for guns were built on the corners, and two small swivel guns from an English ship were mounted on them.

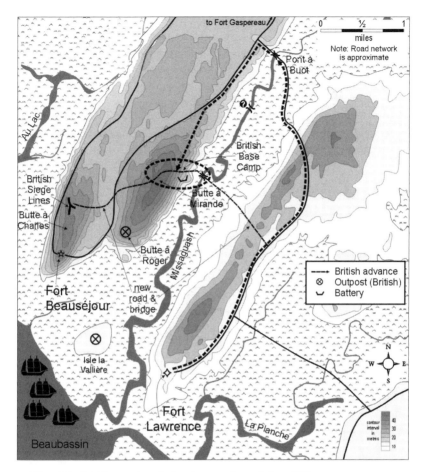

Map of the British operations during the campaign and siege, 1755.

Vergor wanted to destroy both the redoubt and the bridge and draw the nearly two hundred Acadians available in the area directly into defence of the fort. Fiedmont, on the other hand, understood the vital importance of the crossing: the only easily bridgeable site between the basin and the swamps and forest to the north. At this crossing, a smaller force could stop the British. He wanted the redoubt strengthened, with

The British Assault Begins | 55

the trenches dug close to the river and improved with revetments and heavy cannon mounted to command the eastern approaches. But the key improvements never happened, since it was impossible to get the Acadians to work. By the first week of June 1755, it was too late. Barallon burnt the bridge but not the redoubt, which he reinforced by mounting additional swivel guns. There is some evidence that a trench or log breastwork was completed behind the redoubt at the edge of the wood line.

Scarcity of surviving evidence makes pinpointing the exact location of Pont à Buot difficult. Old maps place it at a significant curve in the Missaguash River, just below the point where a small stream called Ruisseau de l'Ours joined the main river. This curve may no longer exist because diking and channelling have significantly changed the river's course. It is possible, however, to still mark the old river bed from modern aerial photos. There appears to be evidence of a large bend or curve in the river just south of the Point de Bute intersection, where two small creeks still flow into the Missaguash. The southernmost creek corresponds more closely to the location of the Ruisseau de l'Ours on both the old maps and sketches. It is possible to gain access to this spot on the Nova Scotia side by following the road that runs north across the Fort Lawrence Ridge to where it changes into a trail that turns towards the river. From here one must proceed on foot and follow a modern dike to the bend in the Missaguash; here is the most likely site of Pont à Buot.

The problem of finding the old bridge site is compounded because, in 1755, the Missaguash River was much wider than it is today and was fully tidal to Point de Bute. Two hundred and fifty years ago, the tides regularly scoured its banks and flushed the silt, so that most of the river was navigable for small vessels for several kilometres inland. This scouring action also made the river a major obstacle to the British. Crossing the river at low tide on foot would have been impossible. The mud and silt have the consistency of glue, and people have been known to get stuck and drown in the fast-rising tide. Moreover, eighteenth-century troops fought and marched in formed ranks. Quite apart from the natural danger, crossing the river on foot would have broken the ranks and destroyed the cohesion of troops, making them extremely vulnerable and ineffective while the thick, clinging mud immobilized them, turning them into easy targets. In fact, in 1756, a British punitive expedition along the Petitcodiac River at Hillsborough was caught on the mud flats and nearly annihilated by French troops. It would also have been nearly impossible for the British to bring their field artillery across without some form of bridge. Even if troops could cross at low tide, they would then be trapped as the river rose behind them. For Monckton and his men, there was only one way over the tidal Missaguash River, and that was by using the Pont à Buot crossing. Consequently, both sides knew where the first shots in the siege of Fort Beauséjour would be fired.

The British Army Advances

On the morning of June 4, 1755, the drums sounded the reveille and the British mustered around Fort Lawrence. The men lined up in column of route in three ranks. Monckton set the following order of march, starting with Provincial scouts:

> A Captain [Captain Adams of Winslow's Battalion], two subalterns and fifty irregulars [Provincial rangers] to scour the woods. Then the Regulars, being about 270 Rank and File. After the regulars, Captain Broome with the detachment of artillery, 4 field six pounders, tumbrels and materials for a bridge. Then followed the 2nd battalion of Irregulars under the Command

of Lieutenant Colonel Scott. The first Battalion under the command of Lieutenant Colonel Winslow bringing up the Rear.

From their ramparts at Beauséjour, the French could see it all. Fiedmont recorded it in his journal. "The English columns extended more than 2,800 yards from van to rear," he wrote; "a few detachments of light troops marched in front and on the flanks. It was estimated that they numbered more than three thousand men." It would have been quite a spectacle, and even today, as one looks across from the walls of Fort Beauséjour towards Fort Lawrence, one can imagine what it would have been like: a column almost three kilometres long, of nearly three thousand men, marching in ranks, colours flying in the middle of their units, and fife and drum marking the cadence. Near the head of the column, sweating volunteers dragged cannon, induced by extra pay and a lack of draught animals, and another detachment of men acting as pioneers marched with pre-cut timber over their shoulders, ready to replace the bridge that they knew the French had destroyed.

Observing the main body of the British force moving north, the French withdrew their observation posts along the Missaguash. The officer in charge of the contingent at Butte à Roger, Ensign M. de Langy, took his twelve men to join the small garrison at Pont à Buot, leaving this post and the one on Tonge's Island unoccupied. Several others joined him from Beauséjour. Ensigns Bailleul and Rouilly from the Canadian (Quebec) companies, Ensign Villeray and cadet Montarville from Louisbourg, and 150 soldiers joined the force covering the Missaguash crossing. Monckton counted about 160 troops leaving the fort as he watched from across the river. Various records suggest that this number is probably too high. That many soldiers would have almost emptied Fort Beauséjour of its uniformed garrison. Probably there were around 200 soldiers at Pont à Buot, mostly Acadians and Natives, with a leavening of regulars. They manned a hastily constructed barricade and

Detail from Lewis Parker's painting, British soldiers at Fort Cumberland (formerly Beauséjour), 1757. *The British camp at Fort Lawrence would have looked much like this on the morning of June 4, 1755, as Monckton's force prepared to march.* LP

the walls of the small redoubt, waiting for the British to appear on the far side of the river.

It took the British approximately four hours to march the six kilometres along the old French road from Fort Lawrence to Pont à Buot, a fairly slow but steady pace. One can walk the same distance today in about an hour and a half. Winslow commented that "progress was slow over the marsh owing to the dikes having been destroyed in places," ruining the road. This would seem to place the actual route itself in dispute. Many writers assume that the road went along the top of the ridge, roughly where it exists today. The diary of John Thomas, a New Englander, suggests this; he says they did not arrive upon the marsh until around eleven o'clock, when they came in full view of the French redoubt. However, if the road was flooded from broken dikes, then

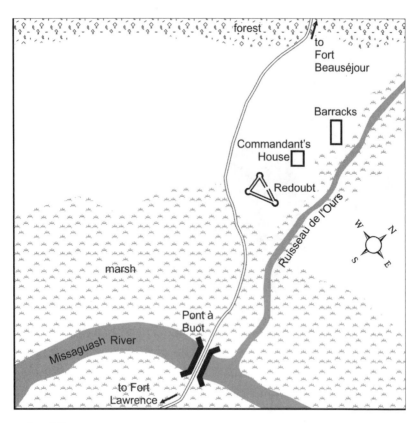

Pont à Buot.

at least part of it had to be at the bottom of the ridge along the edge of the marsh. Some local historians believe that this was in fact the case. They maintain that two roads ran along the base of each side of the Fort Lawrence ridge, since laying a road along the flats involved clearing fewer trees and stumps. According to this interpretation, the British advanced on the eastern side of Fort Lawrence ridge, out of sight of the French, before crossing over the ridge near the Chapman House and moving down towards Pont à Buot across the open marsh. A map drawn by Brewse, a British engineering officer with the expedition, shows just such a route (see page 64).

The British probably arrived at Pont à Buot just before noon. This time is also in dispute; the accounts of Monckton, Winslow, Thomas, and Fiedmont differ. One could assume that Monckton's times were more accurate because, as the senior officer and a man of some social status, he would have the better timepiece. Unfortunately, Monckton did not record the exact time, noting simply that they arrived at the bridge between eleven and twelve.

Upon arrival at the crossing site, the British found the small bridge burnt as expected and the French waiting on the other side. Nonetheless, Pont à Buot was still the best crossing site. The bridge footings remained and a new bridge could be constructed easily — provided that French resistance was not too strong. So the British pressed on, even though the enemy held all the advantage. As Thomas wrote, "We marched direct for the enemy, this being the only pass we could have over to the main fort."

The Battle for Pont à Buot, June 4, 1755

Ensign Barallon's force watched the British approach from behind the walls of their little redoubt and the makeshift barricade. When the British came within range, the Natives let out "their most hideous" battle cry, which apparently terrified the British, while the French and Acadians immediately opened a brisk musket volley and fire from the small swivel guns mounted at the corners of the redoubt. This fire was not very effective. Most of the French musket balls went over the heads of the British vanguard or into the ground in front of them. In fact, the redoubt and barricade were probably too far back from the river to command the eastern side. Eighteenth-century muskets were wildly inaccurate at anything beyond 100 yards — which seems about the distance from the redoubt itself to the river — and the swivel guns were little better. The redoubt was well sited to deal with foot soldiers once they crossed, but, as Fiedmont argued, only cannon could have hurt the British severely as they advanced on the bridge site, and the French had none at Pont à Buot. French fire inflicted only thirteen casualties on the exposed British troops, killing a sergeant, mortally striking two other soldiers, and wounding ten. British infantry responded by quickly putting suppressive volley fire down on the French, and the gunners brought their four six-pounder cannons into action. The French had no effective response to these small field pieces. Within a half an hour, Monckton's cannons destroyed or disabled the swivel guns and set fire to the redoubt.

This was enough for the defenders. The Natives quit the position first and fell back out of cannon range, and most of the Acadians quickly followed suit. Now vastly outnumbered in the face of a determined enemy, the small detachment of French colonial troops soon abandoned the redoubt, set it and the nearby barracks and store building alight, and retired towards Fort Beauséjour. Ensign de Barallon, the senior man on site, had the swivel guns thrown in a bog, and they are probably still there today. The French lost only one soldier, killed by a cannon ball, and two Acadians and a Native chief wounded, but the British had won the battle for the bridge. Thomas was amazed. He found it remarkable that they could have won at so small a cost: "this I think to be the most remarkable thing I ever saw, that we should receive so much fire and nothing to cover us from it, and yet no more killed and wounded, but as we were on the marsh and the enemy on an eminence, they shot over our heads."

Fiedmont believed that the French and their allies fought poorly at Pont à Buot and missed a golden opportunity to stop the British. He

Mid-eighteenth-century artillery, similar to that used by the British in the Beauséjour campaign. This illustration probably shows an 8-inch mortar, which weighed about four hundred kilograms. The field guns resemble those used so decisively at Pont à Buot. MULLER, TREATISE ON ARTILLERY, 1780

was right. The Missaguash crossing was the one place where the French could have reasonably defeated the British plans. If the French had, as Fiedmont suggested, moved out a larger force with heavy cannon and improved the redoubt, with proper trench lines defending the bridge, it was unlikely that the British could have forced a crossing without a more deliberate plan and significantly heavier casualties.

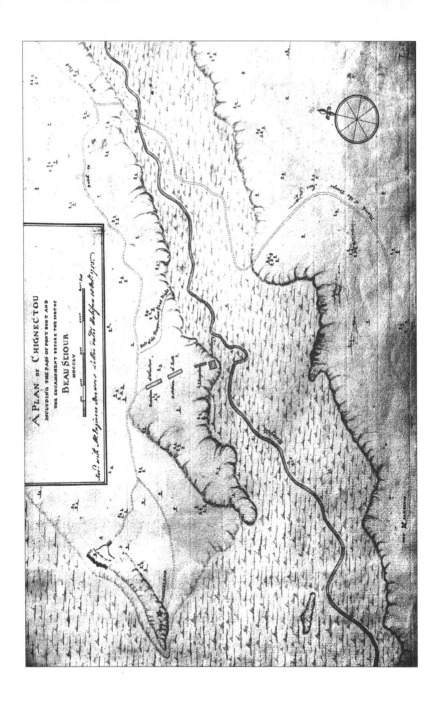

64 | *The Siege of Fort Beauséjour*

Once the French left the post by the river, the British quickly brought forward the provincial pioneers and rebuilt the bridge. After they had crossed, Monckton's force moved a short way along the west edge of the marsh, seizing the high ground around Mount Whatley, where they camped. Things might have been different, but the French had failed to take advantage of the situation at Pont à Buot, and they were never able to recover. From now on they could only react.

Establishment of the British Siege Camp

Monckton took the next several days to consolidate his position on the eastern face of Mount Whatley. "The army encamped on the slope extending from the Missaguash marsh to the top of the hill," Winslow wrote, "the regulars being on a level piece of ground at the foot, the second battalion on the hillside, and the first on top. The road to Butte à Roger was on the right." There is no evidence of this camp today, although artifacts found at Mount Whatley confirm its location. Best guess places it on the northeast side of Mount Whatley, south of the Eddy Road. Not only does this spot fit the descriptions, but it coincides with the likely site of Monckton's new bridge across the Missaguash.

Monckton took steps to make the camp defensible, but he was initially more concerned with making sure he could withdraw to the British side of the river if necessary. He was, after all, now between Fort Beauséjour and Fort Gaspereau at Baie Verte. A French relief force

---

(Opposite) Mr. Brewse's map of the campaign, drawn in Halifax in October 1755, showing the route of march, the crossing of the Missaguash, the camp at Mount Whatley, and the siege lines. The order of encampment at Mount Whatley shows plainly, with Winslow's battalion on the crest of the hill, Scott's below it, and the regulars near the river. The junction of the short road to the siege lines with the main road to the fort is probably the current junction at the Tourism New Brunswick building in Aulac. NAC

arriving at his rear might trap him against the river. To prevent this, he laid a road from the camp to the river, built a dock, and constructed a new bridge over the river at this point in order to shorten the lines of communication with Fort Lawrence. While there are no records that indicate the exact location of the new bridge, descriptions from the journals suggest that the existing bridge over the Missaguash below Mount Whatley is on the site of the original. It makes sense, too, that future British settlers would have made use of Monckton's new bridge, because it shortened the route between the forts; they likely would not have bothered to rebuild a proper bridge at Pont à Buot.

Meanwhile, the French prepared Fort Beauséjour for battle. They scoured the neighbourhood, trying to gather more provisions inside the fort, but little was assembled because the Acadians had kept their carts and wagons to save their own possessions. It was obvious to all that the attack would come from only one direction. The ground above the north side of the fort rises gently upward for about 800 metres to the Acadian village of Butte à Charles, an ideal place for siege artillery because it almost overlooks the fort and is within medium and heavy artillery range. This was the fatal flaw in the fort's design and location. Vergor now ordered the village above the fort burnt, including the church, in order to clear fields of fire.

On June 5, Acadians who had been at Pont à Buot came to the fort. They reported that the British were busy building their second bridge directly below their camp on Mount Whatley. Efforts to improve the fort's defences continued, and the newly arrived Acadians became a much-needed work force. Fiedmont complained that he could not secure enough men to do the work required, having only some thirty soldiers in the artillery service and several Acadians, "the remainder of the garrison — more than one hundred men, merely provided a few sentries." Vergor only exacerbated the manpower problem when he let the Acadians from Pont à Buot return to their homes on the promise that they would continue to harass the British from the woods and "fight in their own way." He also allowed settlers from Baie Verte to return home. When Fiedmont petitioned Vergor to assign more of these men for labour, a count of settlers in the fort came to only 220. This was far less than it should have been — Acadians had either returned to their families or simply hadn't come at all. Fiedmont complained that the Acadians "vanished like smoke"; fewer than half of the 600 men who should have answered the militia call out were present. Officers were sent out to collect the settlers again but returned without success. The Acadians, it was reported, refused to come. They had laid down their arms and thrown away their ammunition, saying they were not disposed to run the risk of being hanged as rebels, as the British had said they would be if they took part in the fighting. As far as most of the Acadians were concerned, the British had already won.

While the French encountered these problems organizing their garrison, the British continued to assemble men and supplies at their quickly growing bridgehead at Mount Whatley. On June 6, they ran several transports up the Missaguash River at high tide to their new dock at the foot of Mount Whatley in order to bring up heavier stores and equipment. Cannon from the fort attempted to stop the vessels, but even the heaviest shot fell well short of the river. A party of troops was then sent out under command of two French Officers, Barallon and Boucherville, to attack the ships from behind the dikes along the river. They were partially successful, and only one of the transports, Sylvanus Cobb's sloop *York*, made it to the British camp on the morning tide, the rest being forced by French musketry to retire. The French sent out another sortie to interdict movements on the evening tide, but this time British infantry met them and forced them to return to the fort, allowing several other small vessels to reach Mount Whatley.

Meanwhile, inside Fort Beauséjour, the French tore down the roofs of their buildings. This lowered the profile of the fort, prevented the roofs from catching cannon shot deflected by the sloped glacis of the fort's walls, and protected against fire. The evening of the June 6, another patrol was organized, and an Acadian woodsman named Beausoliel volunteered to go with a party of Natives to secure a British prisoner.

Consolidation of the British Camp

The British dispatched several reconnaissance patrols of their own that night. It was Monckton's original idea to establish a siege line on Butte à Roger, the spur of the Mount Whatley ridge now intersected by the four-lane highway . When viewed from Fort Lawrence, Butte à Roger looked about the right distance from Fort Beauséjour for a siege battery. The French maintained an observation post on this hill until it, along with their position on Tonge's Island, was abandoned in order to reposition the troops to Pont à Buot. The French never reoccupied either site, and so the British took possession. Thus they consolidated their foothold on the French side of the river; they now controlled the west bank from Pont à Buot to the Cumberland Basin, with detachments guarding the key points at Mount Whatley, Butte à Roger, and Tonge's Island. These three locations dominating the Missaguash River made it possible for the British to run their transports up the river unimpeded by the French. If cannon had been moved further down the slope from Fort Beauséjour to dominate these key sites, the French might have trapped the transports running supplies and heavy equipment up to the British base camp at Mount Whatley. Had they sunk just one vessel in the river, Monckton would have been left with no clear way to bring up his heavy guns. As it was, he did so with ease. Once again, the French lost the opportunity to disrupt the British. But Monckton now found Butte à Roger too far away from the fort for his siege lines; he was forced to revamp his plans.

On June 7, the British brought more transports up the Missaguash and constructed a battery near the unloading point to cover the ships. The small mound on the southwest side of the bridge directly below Mount Whatley is the likely location of this battery, although no evidence has come to light to prove it. Boucherville, one of the French officers sent out to scout the British camp, reported that interdiction of the British ships would now be extremely difficult, because the battery was well sited to sweep the sides of the dikes. The British also completed a breastwork of stumps and branches around the Mount Whatley encampment, making it more defendable. It would seem that Monckton spent an inordinate amount of time and effort in constructing his base camp, but he had no reliable information about the possibility of a French relief force and took that threat seriously.

This threat never materialized because the Royal Navy squadron, dispatched almost a month earlier, cruised on station in the mouth of the St. Lawrence. In fact, on June 8, Admiral Boscawen's fleet intercepted the French off the coast of Newfoundland. The results were less than satisfactory for both sides. Most of the French ships slipped away in a fog, but the fleet was split up, with some ships running for Quebec and others escaping to Louisbourg. Boscawen captured two of the transports and the over three hundred soldiers they were carrying. Having failed to capture or destroy the fleet, Boscawen proceeded to blockade Louisbourg. Nevertheless, his harassment forestalled any aid to the beleaguered garrison of Fort Beauséjour from either Louisbourg or Quebec.

After three days of consolidation, Monckton felt adequately protected and had sufficient supplies and equipment at Mount Whatley to begin the actual siege work. The day Boscawen fought his action off Newfoundland, Monckton set about searching for a location to commence his formal siege of Fort Beauséjour.

A soldier of the 40th Regiment of Foot, one of the British regiments garrisoning Nova Scotia that provided regular troops for the siege. Others came from the 45th Foot and British artillery and engineers. The New Englanders of Shirley's regiment were issued with similar coats of rough cloth. G.A. EMBLETON, PC

CHAPTER FOUR

The Siege
June 8-16, 1755

The first British shells burst inside Fort Beauséjour on June 13, 1755, eleven days after Monckton's soldiers waded ashore through the surf and mud at the mouth of the Missaguash. Monckton's progress had been slow but deliberate. Forcing a crossing of the river at Pont à Buot, consolidating the camp at Mount Whatley, searching for suitable siege lines, and then building a road to move up guns and ammunition took time. So long, in fact, that the French believed the British had redirected their attention towards Fort Gaspereau, at Baie Verte, to sever communications with Louisbourg. The French sent out patrols searching for information, and on June 8 they met the British probing for a suitable location to commence a siege. On that day the battle for the fort itself began in earnest, and it would end suddenly a mere eight days later.

The First Battle of Butte à Charles

The days from June 8 to June 12 were marked by multiple skirmishes and ambushes as the British established themselves on the high ground above the fort and the French tried to prevent the siege lines from being drawn. The first of these days was particularly eventful. With the camp secure, Winslow recorded that Monckton sent out a strong party of Provincials with engineer Captain Tonge (who later settled on Isle la Vallière and gave it his own name) to find ground suitable for the siege line. Monckton reported that Winslow commanded this force but said the engineer was Mr. Brewse (sometimes spelled Bruce) and not Tonge. Little is known about these two men, and the discrepancy and Winslow's failure to mention that he was in command are difficult to reconcile. The answer may be that both engineers went and that Winslow simply did not record that he actually led the party. The diary of John Thomas supports Monckton's report:

> Plesant morning Colonel Winslow marched out of the Camp at 5 o'clock this morning with 360 men, our Company marched In front & as we Came on a Small Emenence a large number of enemy salleyed out of the Foart & fired on us from behind the Stumps & Rocks but we pressed on them with so much vigor that thay were obliged to retreat to the Foart In Great Confusion we took one Prisoner it begins to Rain so that is thought best pickets to Return to ye Camp where we arived P.M. very wet & Feteaged

French accounts suggest why Winslow may have neglected to mention that he commanded the detachment. Fiedmont wrote that on June 8 the French observed the British moving under cover towards the high ground of Butte à Charles between six and seven o'clock that morning, which supports Thomas's departure time of five a.m. It took them an hour to move — cautiously — through the woods from their camp to the high ground above the fort. The French sallied from Beauséjour in an attempt to dislodge the British, and a skirmish ensued: the first Battle of Butte à Charles.

Sometime during this fight, a French raiding party under M. de Beausoliel, the Acadian militiaman, returned with a prisoner, Ensign Hay of the British regulars, captured by Natives while carrying messages between the British encampment at Mount Whatley and Fort Lawrence. From his position in the fort, Fiedmont saw both the skirmish at Butte à Charles and Beausoliel's party, and that they would pass close to one another. The French fired several cannon in an effort to warn Beausoliel's raiding party of the danger that the British would intercept them. According to Fiedmont, there was no way Winslow could not have seen Hay and his captors, and he might have rescued him had the British "wished to sacrifice a few men to our cannon — for no measure had been taken [by the French] to insure the arrival of the prisoner." Perhaps, Fiedmont speculated, the British feared an ambush. "The enemy apparently believed that we had taken this precaution," he wrote, "otherwise, I think they would not have lost so good an opportunity to rescue their officer."

Did Winslow see Ensign Hay and decide it was too risky to attempt a rescue? No one knows. Perhaps Winslow chose not to mention the incident nor his part in it in order to avoid blame. Monckton certainly would have insisted that the Provincials attempt to rescue a regular officer and would have been disappointed if he knew they had failed to do so. It is not known what happened between the two when Winslow returned to the camp, but we do know that the two officers were bitterly divided by the experience of the expedition, and their relationship was marked by contempt and even open hostility.

Beausoliel's raiding party entered the fort around ten o'clock, having successfully avoided the skirmish. Vergor invited Hay to write to

Monckton and his family at Fort Lawrence, informing them that he was safe and well treated. That afternoon Ensign de Barallon carried the letter to the British camp under a flag of truce. Fed and served something to drink, Barallon was allowed to walk about, and he reported that he was told by his escorts that the British had over thirty-two cannons and twenty-two mortars. Although Monckton clearly had more guns than his original list of equipment authorized (twelve 18-pound cannon and several siege mortars of different calibres including at least one 13-inch), Barallon's figure was a wild exaggeration. What Vergor and Fiedmont thought of his report we do not know.

Meanwhile, when the British finally arrived at Butte à Charles, overlooking Fort Beauséjour, they "realized that no more suitable base for their operations could have been found." At forty-two metres above sea level, Butte à Charles was actually the same height as the tops of the walls of the fort some 600 metres to the south. In 1755, the entire area was clear cut, and a man standing on the ramparts could see approximately two hundred metres beyond the crest of Butte à Charles (trees now obscure this view). Monckton had found his spot, but on June 8 he was not yet ready to occupy it, and he ordered everyone back to camp. Another four days of preparation were needed before he could have troops move forward and start digging.

Butte à Charles was Beauséjour's Achilles heel. A reverse slope provided shelter from the French cannon, while from its crest the fort was within easy range of British cannons and mortars. Unfortunately, the exact location of the siege lines has never been found. Fiedmont placed them roughly a thousand yards north of the fort (which seems a little far), and we know that they were within sight and mortar range. Although partially obscured by brush, the tops of the British trenches could apparently be seen from the fort. Fiedmont reports watching the splash of his shot and the collapse of trench walls struck by his cannon balls. However, a contemporary map of the siege suggests that the

British lines were well behind the slope, except perhaps at the extreme western end, and that the first sap forward never reached the crest. The historian J.C. Webster initially confused later British outer works with the 1755 siege lines and published a diagram in his *Historical Guide to New Brunswick* made by the British engineer Tonge that clearly showed the siege lines on the crest. The British immediately filled in the trenches after the siege, and the area has since been farmed, abandoned, and grown over.

The Days of Waiting and Preparation

The British spent June 9 close to their camp at Mount Whatley, building roads and bringing up stores and cannons from the river. Monckton recorded that he was forced to use men to drag the cannon up the hill due to the lack of draught animals — tough and dirty work in the heavy spring rains that hit the isthmus that day. The Chignecto area is exposed to weather from both the Northumberland Strait and the Bay of Fundy, and northeast winds often drive a cold rain horizontally across the marshes. It can become very miserable very quickly. Yorkshiremen who settled in Chignecto in the 1770s described these bitter spring rains as "sheep killers." At Fort Beauséjour the Acadians refused to work because of the rain, and it caused Fiedmont to describe June 9 as "a day even less eventful than those that preceded it" — a curious comment given what had happened on the eighth.

It was still raining the next morning. Even so, the French dispatched a strong party of 150 men under M. de Vannes, with orders to lay an ambush where the British were observed marking the siege lines. The British failed to appear, and after waiting all day, the ambush party returned at dusk, cold and sodden. The British never came forward from their camp at Mount Whatley; they spent June 10 finishing the road from Pont à Buot to the camp and hauling cannon and supplies. Meanwhile, inside Fort Beauséjour, Fiedmont coerced a few Acadians into improving the cannon embrasures, and a courier returned from Fort Menagoueche at the mouth of the St. John River with news that Father Germain, the French missionary, refused to send Native warriors. Beauséjour would fall before they arrived, he said, and Germain was unwilling to leave his post undefended. "This reply caused great surprise" to those in the fort and they sent back a courier to plead with the priest again. The French kept this news from the Acadians for fear that it would ruin their already poor morale.

The rain finally stopped on the eleventh. The French continued to improve the fort's threatened north side with expedient and hasty fortifications with only grudging cooperation from the Acadians. The work progressed slowly, Fiedmont said, adding, "I despaired of achieving the external defence works I had projected." Fiedmont was suspicious of the Acadian willingness to participate in sorties. "It was apparent," he wrote, "that these people were not adapted to harry the enemy, and the repeated sorties they made were a great waste of time." The raids simply provided an opportunity for the Acadians to shirk off into the woods rather than work on the fort. Despite this, Fiedmont continued to make improvements to the curtain face and the tops of the bastions that faced Butte à Charles. He wrote:

> The only defences which had been completed were the platform and blindages [tops of the bastions where the cannons were placed] to protect the curtain which was exposed to attack; the salient angles of the bastions, and the other works were raised to provide cover from enfilading fire from the heights opposite [Butte à Charles]. Part of this was faced with larges casks laid horizontally one upon another and fastened together securely with pins forming coffers which were filled with wood, well

David Coldwell's marvellous model of Fort Beauséjour in 1755, now on display at the fort's museum. The small size of the parade ground in the centre shows clearly in the model, as does the original French gate facing north – and the British attackers. The small building tucked into the bastion on the right is the casemate which collapsed under British fire on June 16. PC

The Siege | 77

beaten earth and other material suitable to withstand cannon balls. The gunners were employed making merlons for the barbette batteries [protective gun emplacements].

At Mount Whatley, the British spent another day unloading and moving supplies from the river. There is no record of the total number of transports that came up the Missaguash, but it may have been as many as two or three on each tide. The small ships had a limited cargo capacity, so each had to make several trips to bring in all the supplies. Again, there are no records available to tell how the transfer was made between the bigger ships in the basin and the smaller sloops, and there are no records of how the fleet was managed during this time. It is reasonable to assume that the majority of the empty transports were allowed to return to Boston or Halifax as a cost-saving measure.

With the break in the weather on June 11, Monckton sent 400 men from Winslow's Battalion forward to scout out a suitable route on which to build a road to the site of the proposed siege lines. This party met no French patrols. In addition, Captain Adams, who led the march from Fort Lawrence, took out a raiding party of Provincial rangers to the former French village near the fort and returned with a "fine coach" that had allegedly belonged to Barallon.

The Second Battle of Butte à Charles

Finally, late in the afternoon of June 12, the British sent around four hundred New Englanders under Lieutenant-Colonel Scott and a company of regulars under Captain Spital to occupy and secure the site for the siege line at Butte à Charles. Another force of around two hundred colonials remained ready to move forward and start digging. Fiedmont recorded that he was surprised it had taken the British so long to make this move, again speculating that they had gone to capture Fort Gaspereau.

But there was no doubting British intent on the twelfth. Having spotted the large British contingent moving towards Butte à Charles, the French sent out a sizable force to meet them. Just how many men left the fort is unclear. Fiedmont estimated 250, but he observed that even the French did not know because they collected the force "without any supervision beyond the mustering of those who wished to shoot at the English under cover of stumps and bushes." The two sides met in battle at Butte à Charles. According to Fiedmont, the British were the first to take the high ground and therefore had the advantage over the French. Monckton reported exactly the opposite: that the French were beaten back by superior numbers and better resolve. He added that Scott conducted himself well, and he also took the opportunity to praise the performance of the regular troops.

Apart from that, we know nothing of the second battle at Butte à Charles on June 12: the exchange was short, cautious, and a British victory. After an hour of trading musket fire, the French retreated. Casualty figures clearly favour the French and lend credence to Monkton's claim that the British drove the French off the high ground and suffered greater losses as a result. Only one Frenchman was killed, and Ensign de Bailleul was wounded. The British lost one regular soldier, while Major Preeble from Winslow's battalion, Captain Tonge, the engineer officer accompanying the party, and four privates were wounded. This casualty rate after an hour of firing also suggests a tentative action between two inexperienced and wary colonial militias. Without Tonge, however, the British could not start digging their siege line; they had to wait for Ensign Peach, a regular officer appointed to act as the engineer, to come forward with 200 workers to commence the siege trenches. Brewse, the other engineer, was still available, but the science of constructing simple siege works would have been part of all regular officers' education and well within Peach's competency to supervise. That night, as Scott's men started breaking ground on the main trench line, Fiedmont fired several "fireballs" on speculation at likely British positions with little effect. Meanwhile, French enthusiasm for nightly sorties withered, now that the British were so close and had commenced the serious siege work.

The Formal Siege Begins

The next morning, June 13, the French watched from the ramparts as the British worked on their trench lines. They had spent a busy night completing their main line and commencing their first sap. What Fiedmont observed was the beginning of the finely choreographed eighteenth-century European siege. Once the attacking force moved within cannon range, they laid out a main position and then began pushing zigzag trenches — saps — forward to establish an advanced gun position parallel to the face of the fort — a "parallel." Here the first heavy siege cannon firing solid cast iron balls were normally deployed, and the attacker tried to batter the fortress, breach the walls, and suppress enemy fire. As the bombardment began, further trenches were pushed forward to create a second parallel, where more cannons and preferably heavy mortars could be mounted; these mortars fired 80-90 kilogram explosive shells in a high trajectory directly into the fort. If necessary, a third parallel was constructed to produce overwhelming fire on the threatened portion of the fort and to furnish an assembly area for the infantry that would make the final assault. In theory, once the mortar bombs began to fall inside the fort, it was all but over for the defenders. The surviving map of the siege suggests that the British completed only one parallel trench and a short section of sap leading to what would have been the second parallel. The eastern end of this trench lay in a reverse

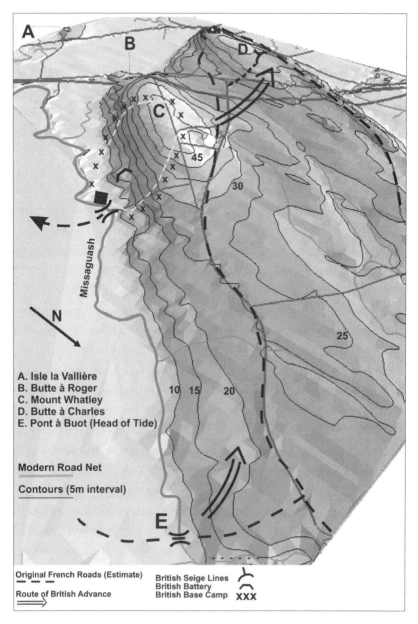

Digital terrain map of the siege. DF, SNB

The Siege | 81

slope, making it an ideal location for mortars. Moreover, the position was already uncomfortably close for the French: even the small 8-inch British mortars could reach Beauséjour from the crest of Butte à Charles.

What Fiedmont saw on the morning of June 13 corresponds roughly with the map of the siege lines: a trench which "appeared to begin at the knoll on the slope of the height," that is, the western end, with the other end hidden in some bushes. He also noted that the British had set up some small mortars in this trench and quickly set his cannons on this new threat. Normally, eighteenth-century fortifications were well protected against cannons, which fired solid shot horizontally. The earth walls of Beauséjour were designed to deflect these shots over the fort or absorb them. But there was no good defence against mortars; the defenders had to prevent them from firing.

The British bombardment started on June 13. Winslow records that at about seven in the morning they brought two small 8-inch mortars and some small artillery — "royals," according to Monckton's account — up to the siege line. Once these were in place, they started bombarding the French with "much difficulty," firing around fifty shells that day. Both Monckton and Winslow commented that this fire was not very effective because the guns were too small. The French perhaps shared that estimation. Although British mortar fire immediately killed an Acadian worker and caused virtually all work on the fortifications to stop, about twenty-five of the more courageous men continued working and helped finish improvements to the fort's gate, which faced Butte à Charles. (The gate was relocated by the British after the siege to its present position). That night, a party of Abenaki arrived and promised to harass the British and take some prisoners; they made a sortie which Fiedmont claimed was unsuccessful. The British defended their siege lines with a picket of fifty men who lay flat on the ground for the night about eighty-five yards out front. At this time, the British ceased their mortar barrage, and the French finally opened fire on the British trenches. Monckton reported that this fire was effective and caused them to abandon work on a part of the trench for the night.

Rain Delay, June 14

Bad weather set in once again the next day, which made digging extremely difficult, and consequently the British did little to improve their siege lines. Likewise, the downpour made work on the fort difficult, although the rain did not seem to prevent the sides from shooting at each other. Here the French records become confusing. Fiedmont opened his entry for June 14 with the comment that they "had no occasion to fire their cannon." This is probably an error in translation or transcription, because Fiedmont later commented that his "artillery continued to check the advance of the enemy's trenches," and he described the ensuing artillery duel with the British. Both Winslow and Thomas corroborate this, commenting on the brisk exchange of fire maintained between the trenches and the fort all day on the fourteenth. Winslow wrote that it was the French who commenced firing on the trenches and that both mortar and cannon fire from the five royals fell short, probably because of damp powder. However, French fire from their larger pieces was accurate and effective, disabling one of the British mortars. It is generally recognized that French gunnery was superior to the British in this era, and, when properly maintained, French artillery had greater range and accuracy; this was the case on June 14 at Beauséjour.

As for the effectiveness of the British bombardment on that day, Fiedmont said that it was minimal. However, he was worried that the British were now using heavier guns, possibly even 12-inch mortars — the standard size of the French heavy mortar. In fact, Monckton had one 13-inch heavy siege mortar, which he sent forward on the fourteenth. But it is not clear if it was actually used that day. Winslow and Thomas both

French fortress artillery. This 18-pounder cannon at the Fort Louisbourg reconstruction is manned by artillerymen of Les Compagnies franches de la Marine. The same troops manned Fort Beauséjour's smaller but similar guns and returned effective fire on the British siege lines. Monckton's attacking force included twelve guns of this size, and the British later mounted some in the fort. PC, FORT LOUISBOURG

recorded that they did not start using the heavier mortar until the next day, the fifteenth, which is probably correct. Fiedmont, who wrote his journal some time after the battle and likely to absolve himself for the fort's eventual capitulation, says that he warned Vergor on June 14 that the casemate where they sheltered could not withstand a heavy mortar bomb.

There is no speculation about the other bad news the French received late on June 14. At about ten o'clock that night, a courier arrived with a message from the governor of Louisbourg: no reinforcements would come because the British squadron under Boscawen was now blockading the harbour. Vergor tried to keep the news a secret, but it quickly spread throughout the fort, revealed (according to tradition) by Vergor's Acadian servant. This caused the majority of the Acadians to lose heart, and Fiedmont recorded that eighty of them disappeared over the wall that night.

Without hope of relief, morale inside Fort Beauséjour plummeted, and heavy rain again on the morning of the fifteenth did not help. One of the soldiers deserted, and many of the Acadians who crowded into the casemates and bunkers refused to work. A spokesman for the settlers said that since there was little hope of relief and even less of defeating the British, they preferred to "abandon" the fort. Other more insidious statements were made. Fiedmont does not tell us what they were, only that the military leadership (with the help of the Abbé Le Loutre) reacted harshly. The commandant forbade any verbal dissent and promised to shoot anyone leaving the fort and then confiscate his family's property. This induced a few to return to improving the fort amid the drenching rain and the continued bombardment.

The Bombardment Renewed, June 15-16

Despite the rain, British mortars and guns renewed their bombardment at daybreak on the fifteenth, and the French replied in kind, disrupting work on the sap that was angling its way towards the fort. Again Fiedmont's journal seems to be a day out of step with the British. He recorded that on the fifteenth he directed fire against the suspected location of the British mortar pit (which indicates that it was in dead ground beyond the crest of the hill) and believed that he was successful in damaging one. He may well have done this with the single mortar listed in the fort's inventory, although surviving accounts do not make this clear. However, British journals record the destruction of one of

The weapon that sealed the fate of Fort Beauséjour: the British 13-inch iron landservice mortar, seen here in action in about 1843. Its massive size and weight (1.6 tonnes) necessitated the building of roads, but its 90 kg shell quickly made the fort untenable. DETAIL FROM A PRINT BY CAMPION

their mortars the day before. In addition, both Winslow and Thomas wrote that the fifteenth was the first day they used the heavier 13-inch mortar, casting further doubt on Fiedmont's earlier remarks that he had witnessed larger bombs on the fourteenth.

That night, in what had become their routine, the British rearranged the troops in the trenches. They were kept busy by a small force of Natives and Acadians, who harassed their pickets and outposts throughout the night. Consequently, they were unable to further develop the forward trenches and had to wait until the morning.

As soon as it was light on the sixteenth, the British started digging again, but Fiedmont claims that he was able to drive them off with his cannons. This suggests that the sap had crested the hill and was plainly visible from the fort. French fire prompted a response from the British, who commenced an intense shelling of the fort with both the heavy and light mortars and the small cannons. It was this exchange of fire that unexpectedly forced the French to surrender. Just before nine o'clock, one of the heavy 13-inch mortar bombs exploded on the roof of the casemate used by the French officers. Based on archeological work that recovered some destroyed and crushed French artifacts, it is widely accepted that this bunker was located in the northwest bastion, on the west side of the French gate. Fiedmont had specifically mentioned that this bunker was incapable of withstanding the larger bombs, but his warnings were ignored. Consequently, when the bomb exploded and collapsed the roof of the bunker, it caught some of the French officers and the British prisoner, Ensign Hay, eating breakfast. The blast killed six people outright: Ensign Raimbault, the interpreter; M. Ferand, the clerk; M. Billy; two Acadian servants; and Ensign Hay. Another two officers were injured.

Despair Inside the Fort

The destruction of the casemate shattered the already poor morale of the garrison and "increased the disorder in the fort." No place within the tiny fortress was safe from the power of the heavy mortar. The defender's will to fight was broken. Le Loutre, who had never left the confines of the fort since the arrival of the British, tried one last time to cajole and intimidate his flock, vehemently opposing any talk of capitulation and saying that it was better to be buried in the ruins of the fort than to give it up. But his hold over the Acadians was gone, and they

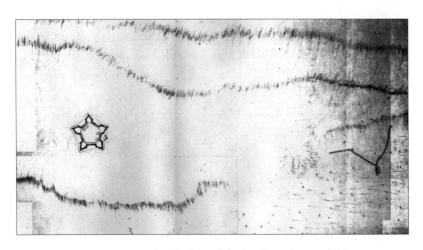

A contemporary British sketch of the fort and the siege lines, showing the first position and the sap moving forward for the parallel (never begun) on the crest of the slope. The gun position at the base of the siege lines seems to hold three mortars. NAC

went to Vergor demanding that he seek favourable terms with the British. If he did not do so, they threatened to overwhelm the garrison and deliver the fort to the British themselves. It is highly unlikely that they could have done this without support from the soldiers, because by this time their numbers were roughly equal. However, no record mentions an impending mutiny among the French garrison.

Nonetheless, the commandant quickly held a council of war with his remaining officers. Everyone was concerned about the capability of the remaining bunkers and bomb-proofs to withstand the heavier bombs. Vergor was particularly concerned about the powder and ammunition bunker and Fiedmont would not vouch for the safety of the magazine. Although the powder room had been designed to withstand a French 12-inch bomb, the British 13-inch (90 kg) bomb was more destructive, and the room would not likely stand up to repeated attacks. "No part of the fort, however, was considered safe from bombs," Fiedmont wrote;

"the bomb which had destroyed the casemate had thrown down the curtain alongside it; the garrison was too weak to withstand the threats of the settlers; the fort, furthermore, was not capable of the least resistance; there was no hope of help, and still less of holding the post."

Surrender, June 16

That was it. Vergor agreed to surrender the fort and seek the most honourable terms he could. At about nine o'clock in the morning, the British saw a flag of truce rise over the ramparts. M. de Vannes brought a letter to the British lines requesting a forty-eight-hour ceasefire in order to negotiate a surrender. He was taken to Monckton at Mount Whatley and delivered the letter at about noon. Monckton apparently was surprised. He did not think that Fort Beauséjour would capitulate so quickly. They had barely begun the siege and not even encircled the fort, and in fact, contrary to what Mary Beacock Fryer wrote in *Battlefields of Canada*, Monckton never had sufficient troops or time to invest the fort entirely.

As a result of this apparently hasty capitulation, Monckton had a low opinion of the French defenders and contemptuously gave Vannes only two hours to return with suitable terms. Vergor quickly drafted the proposed terms of capitulation, and Vannes went back to the British camp. This time M. Bouilly, who would act as a hostage in good faith, accompanied him. Vannes arrived in the British camp at the appointed time and handed the proposal over to Monckton.

There are variations in translations of the terms of capitulation printed in John Clarence Webster's pioneering publications on the Beauséjour story (see Bibliography, page 103). The following ten terms proposed by Vergor are taken from Fiedmont's journal, which was translated by Alice Webster, J.C. Webster's remarkable wife, in 1936.

1. The Commandant, Officers, staff in the service of the King, and the Garrison of Beauséjour, to march out with arms, baggage, drums beating, fuses burning;

2. The Commandant shall have at the head of the garrison six cannon of the largest calibre, one mortar, and fifty charges for each piece;

3. His Britannic Majesty shall furnish supplies necessary for the transport of this force to Baie Verte, where the garrison will embark in a French vessel to go wheresoever they please;

4. The garrison shall take with it 200 quarters of flour and 100 of bacon;

5. The necessary time to go from this post to Baie Verte and from Baie Verte to their destination shall be accorded the garrison;

6. The Acadians shall not be molested for having taken arms for they were forced to do so under pain of death, and no injury shall be done them;

7. The Acadians are free to enjoy their own religion, to have priests, and no constraint shall be placed upon them;

8. Such Acadians, as desire to do so, shall be permitted to withdraw to the territory of the King of France, and shall be allowed a year, counting from the day of this capitulation, in which to reach a decision;

9. During this year the French shall be permitted to provide the Acadians with the means for their withdrawal; and

10. All the articles of Capitulation, which may be expressed in an obscure manner, shall be interpreted to the advantage of the French and executed in good faith.

Monckton's Five Terms

Monckton found the French terms unacceptable, and he prepared his own, in accordance with his instructions from Governor Lawrence. Given the rather poor defence and the lack of commitment displayed by the French, Monckton saw no reason to be lenient and no necessity to compromise. It is interesting that Monckton omitted all of the articles concerning the welfare of the Acadians except the sixth, and he denied Vergor permission to carry out extra weapons, equipment, supplies, or cannon.

1. The Commandant, staff officers in the King's service, and the Garrison of Beauséjour shall march out with their arms, baggage, and drums beating;

2. The Garrison shall be sent directly to Louisbourg at the expense of the King of Great Britain;

3. The Garrison shall have sufficient provisions to last until their arrival at Louisbourg;

4. The Acadians, inasmuch as they were forced to take up arms under pain of death, shall be pardoned for the part they have taken; and

5. The Garrison shall not bear arms in America during a period of six months.

Sometime after two o'clock, a party of Acadians and Natives attacked the rear of the Mount Whatley encampment. This group had been sent out several days earlier and were not aware that a ceasefire was in effect. The British responded by reinforcing their perimeter and by dispatching a force to counter this new threat. After a brief skirmish, the French force disappeared into the woods, and the British returned with a wounded Native chief who subsequently died. This seems to have been an isolated incident and did not affect the negotiations. Bouilly stayed in the British camp, and an English officer was sent with Vannes to the fort with the new terms at around six o'clock. Monckton gave Vergor an hour to respond, after which these terms would no longer be considered valid.

Upon receiving these new terms, Vergor sent Vannes back to Mount Whatley requesting more time to consider them. Some accounts have it that Monckton did not even read the letter and simply dismissed Vannes. Unfortunately, Monckton did not bother to record any of this. On the way back, Vannes was apparently taken through the trenches and shown the mortars and cannons in an effort to impress and intimidate him. By one account, Vannes was also given food and drink and was quite drunk when he returned to Fort Beauséjour.

At this point the time lines in the journals become confusing again. According to Fiedmont, at seven o'clock, the British started shelling the fort again. He recorded that the British commander at the trenches had orders to recommence firing at this time, and since he had not received any counter-instruction from Monckton, he did so. Oddly, none of the British journals confirm this, and it is difficult to ascertain if it actually happened. Nonetheless, the French held another council and accepted the British terms. It was evident to all that they had no choice. Fiedmont wrote:

In view of the impossibility of receiving help, the letter from M. Drucour [the Governor of Louisbourg], the weakness of the garrison, the insecurity of the casemates, especially the powder magazine, etc., almost all were in favour of accepting the Capitulation.

He then said that, having accepted the terms, the British took procession the fort at seven-thirty, an unlikely claim, since not enough time had elapsed in which to pass the news, let alone allow the British to organize and dispatch a force.

In fact, none of the surviving records match at this stage, and it is unclear when the French delivered the surrender, when Monckton accepted it, and when the British actually entered and took possession of Fort Beauséjour. In any case, all agree that possession took place at around dusk. Monckton sent in a regular detachment and the Provincial battalion under Lieutenant-Colonel Scott, who was the first to enter the fort. By then only troops of the Compagnies franches de la Marine remained; the Acadians and the priest Le Loutre had slipped out before the British arrived.

The British found Beauséjour in horrible shape. The buildings had been destroyed by the shelling, and none of the damaged bunkers or walls had been repaired. Stores and provisions littered the small parade square. The French attempted to categorize the items for the British, but all discipline soon vanished, the French troops started pillaging, and a drunken frenzy ensued. Fiedmont says that the British, who initially only manned the ramparts, participated in the mayhem, but no one else claims this. The French continued looting all night, and it proved impossible for the British to obtain an inventory of the fort's property. The next morning, June 17, 1755, the French garrison of 160 marched out of the fort and into camps to await their transport.

The Surrender of Fort Gaspereau

Monckton renamed Beauséjour Fort Cumberland, in honour of the Duke of Cumberland, who was the commander of the British Army and his patron. Some of the cannon fired a salute to mark the occasion. The British found that many of the fort's twenty-one cannons were in poor condition, and two had split when they were fired because they were so badly rusted. That same day, Monckton sent a letter to the Commandant of Fort Gaspereau, Captain Benjamin Rouer de Villeray, offering him the same terms as those given to Vergor and giving him a day to respond.

On the eighteenth, as the British began filling in their siege lines (standard practice to keep any potential relief force from using the line of siege trenches against the victors), Monckton sent Winslow with a detachment of 250 men to take Fort Gaspereau. Winslow followed the Old French Road along the spine of the Beauséjour ridge to Baie Verte. Evidence of this road across the isthmus still exists, and it is said to be used as a snowmobile trail. However, the four-kilometre boardwalk or planked road across the marsh at Baie Verte has long since rotted away and its path forgotten. Winslow found Villeray willing to capitulate to the same terms as Fort Beauséjour. With only twenty-three men and a fort in sad disrepair (being more of a warehouse than a fort), a quick capitulation was his only sensible course of action. Winslow renamed the place Fort Monckton and sent word back to Fort Cumberland that the task was complete.

Transports from Halifax arrived in the Cumberland Basin on June 23, following a remarkably fast passage, to take Beauséjour's French garrison to Louisbourg. With the French safely gone from the isthmus and the forts securely in British hands, Monckton dispatched Rous to capture the remaining French fort at the mouth of the St. John River. Its commandant, Charles des Champs de Boishebert, had received word that Beauséjour had fallen. Without sufficient forces to withstand a siege, Boishebert abandoned and burnt his fort and then retired up the river. Rous did not pursue Boishebert immediately, an oversight the British would later regret.

On July 2, the sloop *Vulture* brought news to Monckton that Rous had successfully completed his task. All the French forts on the isthmus and along the Bay of Fundy had been captured or destroyed. Monckton had executed Lawrence's instructions of February 29, 1755, to the letter, with the loss of only twenty men killed and twenty wounded. The siege of Fort Beauséjour had lasted fifteen days, from the landing of the expedition to the capitulation, and it ended with astonishing quickness.

Fort Beauséjour today, seen from the north. The basic French star plan remains, but the gate has been relocated, and the outer works have been redeveloped, including an extended work to the south, where the museum now stands. PC

CHAPTER FIVE

Peoples and Empires in the Balance

The French never recovered from the loss of Fort Beauséjour. Its capture by the British and the loss of its satellite forts at Baie Verte and on the St. John River had severe military, political, and economic repercussions for all of New France. By some estimates, about a fifth of the entire French population in North America lived in Acadia, and that population was now completely at the mercy of the British. Moreover, Acadia was a major source of food for the region. Maple syrup and maple sugar, wheat, barley, flax, corn or native maize, fruits (particularly apples), vegetables, sheep, goats, and cattle were all exported to Canada and even New England. It is reasonable to assume that the loss of Acadian produce alone had a direct economic impact on France's ability to adequately provision its remaining garrisons in New France, particularly Fortress Louisbourg.

The loss of Fort Beauséjour also struck a severe blow to French influence among key Native allies in the region. These tribes supported the French throughout the Seven Years War that started officially in 1756, and they actively participated in the long guerrilla-style war against the British in New Brunswick. Even so, without continuous French support — and a sympathetic Acadian population to draw upon — their ability to disrupt the British colonization of the region was over.

But most importantly, the fall of Fort Beauséjour cleared the way for a major readjustment of the settlement pattern of the whole Atlantic region. Successive Nova Scotia governors had attempted to administer the oath of allegiance to their Acadian subjects but had always failed because the Acadians constantly refused to agree to any stipulation regarding the bearing of arms. They steadfastly insisted on their right to remain neutral in case of war between Great Britain and France. The British, in turn, refused to acquiesce on the point of neutrality and insisted on full compliance. Acadian involvement in the defence of Fort Beauséjour entirely compromised the neutrality of at least the Chignecto Acadians, but Lawrence offered them one more chance to accept the unconditional oath. The Acadian representatives completely misread the situation and once again attempted to play the neutrality card. This tactic backfired, and Lawrence ordered the deportation of all Acadians to New England, where it was hoped that they would be quickly assimilated.

Le Grand Dérangement remains one of the most controversial events in Canadian history. Monckton assigned the duty of deporting the Acadians to his Provincial corps — the New Englanders. Some New Englanders, especially the Rangers, who were experienced in the grim realities of frontier wars, took to the task of expulsion with zeal, and atrocities occurred. Most, however, found it thoroughly disagreeable: as

Winslow observed uneasily, it "will look odd in history." He was right. But Winslow and his men did as they were ordered with as much civility as the circumstances permitted, and many Acadian families were loaded onto ships below the walls of the fort that had failed to save them. Less than a decade later, their lands along the Bay of Fundy were occupied by New England settlers.

The campaign also had implications for relations between the British and their American colonists. The whole Beauséjour expedition fanned the animosity that already existed between the British and the Provincials. In one incident, Winslow had his regimental colours publicly taken from him, an insult to any soldier. Monckton added to the insult when his official report to Lawrence failed to mentioned the Provincial contribution and gave the impression that the whole affair was accomplished by British regulars. Governor Lawrence's own report to London echoed that assessment, and accusations of conspiracy rang throughout Massachusetts when copies of his letter were made public. New Englanders believed that their contribution was ignored and that they were deprived of the credit, just like they had been when they captured Louisbourg in 1745. An article published by Benjamin Franklin in July 1756, during the recruitment for the Crown Point expedition, summarized this resentment:

> The provincials apprehend that regulars joined with them would claim all the honour of any success and charge them with the blame of every miscarriage. They say that last year, at Nova Scotia, 2,000 New England men and not more than 200 regulars were joined in the taking of Beauséjour; yet it could not be discovered by the account sent home by Governor Lawrence that there was a single New England man concerned in the affair.

The French, too, were not without controversy. In 1757, Vergor was tried in Quebec City for the lacklustre defence of his fort. The trial was a farce. Bigot, the Intendant, swung into action and bribed the court. Vergor was acquitted and reassigned to Louisbourg, which fell to General Wolfe's assault in 1758 — the second of the key French forts to fall to an amphibious attack. When Wolfe's army besieged Quebec in 1759, Vergor commanded a small company at an outpost guarding L'Anse au Foulon, where a pathway led from the St. Lawrence River to the plains above the city. It was there, on the morning of September 13, 1759, that Wolfe's army surprised the guard and scaled the cliff, which led to the battle of the Plains of Abraham and the fall of Quebec. Vergor retired to France in 1761 on an army pension.

Jacau de Fiedmont and Robert Monckton fought at Quebec in 1759 as well. True to form, Fiedmont was one of the few who advocated defending the citadel to the last following the French defeat in the battle on the Plains of Abraham. This valiant Canadien gunner ended his days as governor of French Guiana. Robert Monckton, a solid and dependable soldier, commanded one of Wolfe's brigades at Quebec. It was his troops who surprised Vergor's company at L'Anse au Foulon. After capturing Martinique and serving briefly as governor of New York, Monckton retired to Britain to a successful career as a businessman and member of parliament. John Winslow remained active in the army until 1757; then, following the British disaster at Crown Point, he retired to Massachusetts, where he served in the legislature and judiciary. The Abbé Le Loutre was captured by the British while en route to France in the fall of 1755 and spent the next eight years imprisoned on the Isle of Jersey.

Historians tend to dismiss the siege of Fort Beauséjour as a local affair, one that determined the fate of the Acadians and confirmed British control over what is now Nova Scotia and New Brunswick. Indeed, most interpretations of the importance of the fort and its hinterland derive from continentalist views developed after the advent of

The author, in the light ball cap on the left, leading a group of University of New Brunswick students through Fort Beauséjour, September 2002. The brick casemate in the background, built by the British after 1755, is on the site of the original French gate. NBMHP

railways, views which see the Atlantic provinces as peripheral and unimportant to the main story of interior settlement. For the colonial period, however, nothing could be further from the truth. Beauséjour guarded not only a prosperous and readily accessible agricultural region, it secured overland communications for the French empire in North America. Without access to the river and portage routes through what is now New Brunswick, it is difficult to see how any communications could be maintained between France and the St. Lawrence for roughly half the year. The great imperial fortress at Louisbourg was not sited to do that; indeed its principle role was to secure the fishery — itself far more valuable to France than all the furs of Canada. In fact, when the British were forced to defend Canada and Nova Scotia in the aftermath of the American Revolution against the threat from the south, they moved quickly to occupy and defend present-day New Brunswick because of the key role it played in imperial communications. Loyalist regiments were settled along the St. John River to guard the route, and over the nineteenth century a series of fortresses and blockhouses were built to secure it.

It hardly seems possible that the curious star-shaped, weather-beaten ramparts of that old fortification at Beauséjour could have been a strategic crossroads. Viewed from the wind-swept bastions, it seems an improbable site for a battle that decided the fate of the entire region, the fortune of a people, and perhaps the destiny of an entire continent. But in its time, Fort Beauséjour defended vital ground. The siege of 1755 marked the opening shots of a war that ended the French Empire in North America, reshaped the settlement patterns of the Atlantic region, and laid the groundwork for the modern province of New Brunswick.

SELECTED BIBLIOGRAPHY

Primary Sources

COURVILLE, LOUIS DE. *Memoires sur le Canada*. Societe Litteraire et Historique de Quebec. Quebec: Middleton and Lawson, 1873.

DE FIEDMONT, JACAU; John Clarence Webster, trans. and ed. *The Siege of Beauséjour*. Historical Studies No. 1. Saint John: New Brunswick Museum, 1936.

PICHON, THOMAS. *Thomas Pichon: An Impartial Frenchman. Genuine Letters and Memoires*. London: J. Nourse, 1760.

ROBINEAU DE VILLEBON, JOSEPH; John Clarence Webster, trans. and ed. *Acadia at the End of the Seventeenth Century*. Saint John: New Brunswick Museum, 1934.

WEBSTER, JOHN CLARENCE, ed. *The Journal of Abijah Willard, 1755*. Saint John: New Brunswick Historical Society, No. 13, 1930.

_____. *The Journal of Joshua Winslow*. Historical Studies No. 2. Saint John: New Brunswick Museum, 1936.

_____. *The Journals of Beauséjour: Diary of John Thomas and the Journal of Louis de Courville*. Special publication of the Public Archives of Nova Scotia. Sackville: Tribune Press, 1937.

Secondary Sources

AKINS, THOMAS, ed. *Acadia and Nova Scotia: Documents Relating to the Acadian French and the First British Colonization of the Province, 1714-1758*. Halifax: Charles Annand, 1869.

ANDERSON, FRED. *Crucible of War*. New York: Knopf, 2000.

BIRD, WILL R. *A Century at Chignecto*. Toronto: Ryerson, 1928.

_____. *Done at Grand Pré*. Toronto: Ryerson, 1955.

BOURINOT, J.G. "Some Old Forts by the Sea." Paper delivered to the Royal Society of Canada, Moncton, 1883.

BRUN, REGIS. *Fort de Beauséjour*. Moncton: Éditions d'Acadie, 1993.

DAIGLE, J.M. CYR, and G.ARSENAULT. *Le Fort de Beauséjour*. Moncton: Éditions d'Acadie, 1993.

FILTEAU, GERARD. *Par la Bouche de mes canons!*. Quebec: Septentrion, 1990.

FYTCHE, MARIE AMELIA. *The Rival Forts: The Velvet Siege*. Halifax: A. McNeil, 1907.

McISSAC, J.R. *The Isthmus of Chignectou*. MA Thesis. Wolfville: Acadia University, 1937.

PARKMAN, FRANCIS. *Montcalm and Wolfe*. London: Collier-MacMillan, 1962.

POTHIER, BERNARD. *Battle for the Chignecto Forts*. Toronto: Balimuir, 1995.

SHEWEN, E.T.P. "Notes of Fort Monckton." Dominion Archives: Department of Public Works. Reading from the Chignecto Historical Society, 9 July 1892.

THOMAS, GERALD ARTHUR. *John Clarence Webster: The Evolution and Motivation of an Historian*. MA Report. Fredericton: University of New Brunswick, 1990.

WEBSTER, JOHN CLARENCE. *The Forts of Chignecto*. Shediac: John Clarence Webster, 1930.

_____. *Thomas Pichon: The Spy of Beauséjour*. Sackville: Tribune Press, 1937.

_____. *The Building of Fort Lawrence in Chignecto*. Saint John: New Brunswick Museum, 1941.

_____. *Historical Guide to New Brunswick*. Saint John: New Brunswick Government Bureau of Information and Tourist Travel, 1944.

INDEX

40th Regiment of Foot. *See* British Army, Regulars, 40th Regiment of Foot
45th Regiment of Foot. *See* British Army, Regulars, 45th Regiment of Foot
84th Regiment of Foot. *See* Royal Highland Emigrants

A
Abenaki 10, 82
Acadia 12-22, 32, 36, 45, 97
Acadians 12-20, 21, 25, 27, 28, 31-35, 42-43, 44, 50, 53, 54, 55, 56, 58, 61-62, 66, 67, 68, 75, 76, 85, 86, 87, 90-92, 93, 98-100
Adams, Captain 57, 78
Albany 48
American Revolution 102
Anglo-Mi'kmaq war 15, 28, 33

B
Baie Verte, NB 12, 25, 54, 65, 67, 71, 90, 94, 97
Bailleul, Ensign de 58, 79
Barallon, Ensign de 54, 56, 61, 62, 67, 74, 78
battles
  Butte à Charles, First 72-75
  Butte à Charles, Second 78-80
  Plains of Abraham 100
  Pont à Buot 61-65
Bay of Fundy 11, 12, 13, 19, 25, 28, 34, 37, 42, 43, 47, 75, 95, 99
Beaubassin, NS. *See* Fort Lawrence, NS
Beauséjour, NB 14, 16, 17, 19, 20, 21, 22, 37, 38, 42, 45, 47, 102
Beausoliel, M. de 68, 73
Bigot, François 45-46, 100
blockade 36
Boishébert, Charles des Champs de 94
Boscawen, Vice-Admiral Edward 36, 69, 84
Boston, MA 37, 38, 41, 42, 47, 51, 53, 78
Boucherville, M. de 67, 69
Bouilly, M. 89, 92
Braddock, General Edward 36
Brewse (Bruce), John 61, 65, 72, 79
British Army, Provincial Forces
  New England Irregulars 39
  New England volunteers 41, 45, 51, 52, 53, 59, 78, 98

105

British Army, Regulars
    40th Regiment of Foot 43, 53, 70
    45th Regiment of Foot 43, 53
    Lascelles's Regiment 20
    Warburton's Regiment 20
Broome, Captain 57
Butte à Charles, NB 25, 49, 50, 66, 76, 78-80, 82
Butte à Mirande, NB. *See* Mount Whatley, NB
Butte à Roger, NB 49, 52, 58, 65, 68

C

Cape Breton, NS 12, 13, 15, 36, 52
Chignecto Isthmus 13, 16-28, 39
Chignecto, NS 13, 15, 16, 37, 38, 39, 43, 46, 47, 53, 75, 98
Chipudy, NB. *See* Shepody, NB
Cobb, Sylvanus 46, 50, 67
Coldwell, David 77
Compagnie franches de la Marine. *See* French Army, Compagnie franches de la Marine
Cornwallis, Edward 15, 16, 17, 18-20, 28, 31, 32
Courville, Louis De 19
Crown Point, NY 100
Cumberland Basin 11, 20, 43, 46, 48, 68, 94
Cumberland, Duke of 94

D

Delkekondiak, NB. *See* Petitcodiac, NB
Drucour, Augustin de Boschenry de 93
Duchambon, Louis Du Pont 45

E

England. *See* Great Britain

F

Ferand, M. 87
Fiedmont, Jacau de 46, 50, 52, 53, 55, 58, 61, 62, 66, 67, 72, 73, 74, 75, 76, 78, 79, 80, 82, 83, 84, 85, 86, 87, 88, 89, 92, 93, 100
Five Fathoms Hole 47
Fort Carillon, NY 22
Fort Cumberland, NB 11, 14, 19, 20, 21, 32, 34, 47, 59, 94
Fort Duquesne, PA 17, 22, 36
Fort Gaspereau, NB 25-27, 31, 38, 65, 71, 79, 94
Fort Gediaque, NB. *See* Skull Island, NB
Fort Lawrence, NS 13, 21, 22, 27, 29, 33, 36, 42, 46, 47-48, 50-52, 53, 54, 57-60, 66, 68, 73, 74, 78
Fort Lawrence Ridge, NS 56
Fort Menagoueche, NB 11, 25, 76
Fort Monckton, NB 94
Fort Niagara, NY 17, 22
Fort Rouille, ON 17
Fortress Louisbourg, NS 11-13, 15, 17, 27, 33, 34, 36, 37, 42, 45, 53, 58, 69, 71, 84, 91, 93, 94, 97, 99, 100, 101
France 12, 13, 20, 32, 33, 35, 45, 90, 97-98, 100-101
Franklin, Benjamin 99
French Army
    Compagnie franches de la Marine 19, 30, 45, 50, 84, 93
Fryer, Mary Beacock 89
Fundy National Park 47

G

Galissonnière, Roland Michael Barrin, Comte de la 18

Gaspereau River 25
Germain, Father 76
Grand Manan Island, NB 42
Grand Pré, NS 14
Great Britain 12, 19, 28, 91, 98, 100

H

Halifax, NS 15, 20, 34, 43, 48, 53, 65, 78, 94
Hancock, Merchant 38
Hay, Ensign 73, 87
Hillsborough, NB 57
Hopson, Peregrine Thomas 31, 33
Hudson River 36
Hussey, Captain 46

I

Indian Island, NB. *See* Skull Island, NB
Isle la Vallière, NB. *See* Tonge's Island, NB
Isle St. John. *See* Prince Edward Island

K

Kennebec River 41
Kennebecasis River 25
King George's War. *See* War of Austrian Succession

L

La Corne, Chevalier Pierre 14, 19-20
Lake Champlain 36
Lake Ontario 17
Lake Simcoe 17
Lake Temiscouata 12
Langy, Ensign M. de 52, 58
L'Anse au Foulon, QC 100

Lascelles's Regiment. *See* British Army, Regulars, Lascelles's Regiment
Lawrence, Charles 20, 33, 34, 36, 37, 38-42, 47, 48, 91, 95, 98, 99
Le Loutre, Abbé Jean-Louis 20, 32, 33, 35, 85, 87, 93, 100
Lery, Sieur de 19
London, England 31, 34, 36, 37, 99
Loyalists 102

M

Maine 13, 41, 42
Maliseet 10
Marshfield, MA 41
Mascarene, Paul 13
Massachusetts 15, 27, 28, 36, 41, 99, 100
Memerancoug, NB. *See* Memramcook, NB
Memramcook, NB 18
Mermaid 42
Mi'kmaq 10, 14, 15, 28, 32, 33
Minas Basin 12, 39, 47
Missaguash River 16, 20, 25, 27, 28, 32, 34, 50, 52, 54-57, 58, 63, 65-66, 67, 68, 69, 71, 78
Monckton, Lieutenant-Colonel Robert 11, 37, 38-41, 43, 46, 48, 51, 53-54, 57, 58, 59, 61, 62, 65, 66, 68, 69, 71, 72, 73, 74, 75, 78, 79, 82, 83, 89, 91-95, 98, 99, 100
Montarville, Cadet 58
Mount Whatley, NB 52, 54, 65-69, 71, 73, 75, 78, 89, 92
Murray, Captain 42

N

Nerepis, NB 17

New Brunswick 6, 12, 13, 18, 100-102
New England 28, 34, 36, 41, 42, 97, 98-99
New France 12, 13, 17, 18, 25, 45, 97
New Hampshire 36
New Ireland. *See* New Brunswick
New York 36, 100
New York, NY 38
Newfoundland 69
Northumberland Strait 13, 37, 38, 75
Nova Scotia 10, 12-16, 17, 18, 20, 28-29, 31-34, 36, 37, 41, 42-43, 54, 56, 70, 98-100, 102

O
Ohio River 22, 36

P
Parker, Lewis 33, 59
Peach, Ensign 79
Petitcodiac, NB 18
Petitcodiac River 12, 17, 25, 57
Pisiquid, NS. *See* Windsor, NS
Placentia, NL 45
Point de Bute, NB 25, 54-65, 66, 68, 71, 76
Pont à Buot, NB. *See* Point de Bute, NB
Port Elgin, NB 27
Port Royal, NS 12
Preeble, Major 79
Prince Edward Island 13

Q
Quebec 11, 13, 15, 19, 27, 35, 36, 40, 58, 69, 100

Quebec City, QC 100

R
Raimbault, Ensign 87
Rouilly, Ensign 58
Rous, Captain John 20, 42, 47, 48, 94, 95
Royal Navy 42, 69
Ruisseau de l'Ours, NB 56

S
Ste. Anne's Point, NB. *See* Fredericton, NB
St. Croix River 28
St. John River 11, 17, 18, 20, 25, 31, 39, 76, 94, 97, 102
St. Lawrence River 13, 36, 69, 100, 101
Scott, Lieutenant-Colonel George 41, 46, 51, 53, 58, 65, 78, 79, 80, 93
Sereh 42
Seven Years War 98
Shediac Bay 17
Shediac, NB 26
Shediac River 17
Shepody, NB 18
Shirley, William 15, 36, 37, 39, 41, 42
Shubenacadie, NS 32
Skull Island, NB 17
Spital, Captain 78
Success 42, 46

T
Tantramar River 19, 47
Thomas, John 59, 61, 62, 72, 83, 86
Tintramar River. *See* Tantramar River
Tonge, Captain 72, 75, 79

Tonge's Island, NB 52, 58, 68, 72
Treaty of Aix-la-Chapelle 14
Treaty of Utrecht 12, 32

U

University of New Brunswick 101

V

Vannes, M. de 75, 89, 92
Vergor, Marquis Louis Du Pont
 Duchambon de 11, 22, 26, 35,
 42, 45-46, 47, 48, 50, 53, 55, 66,
 67, 73, 74, 84, 85, 88, 89, 91-94,
 100
Villeray, Captain Benjamin Rouer de
 94
Villeray, Ensign 58
Vulture 46, 95

W

War of Austrian Succession 14, 32
Warburton's Regiment. *See* British
 Army, Regulars, Warburton's
 Regiment
Webster, Alice 89
Webster, J.C. 75, 89
Willard, Abijah 51
Windsor, NS 39
Winslow, Lieutenant-Colonel John
 27, 41, 46, 50-51, 53, 57, 58, 59,
 61, 65, 72-73, 78, 79, 82, 83, 86,
 94, 99, 100
Wolfe, General James 100

Y

York 46, 67

NEW BRUNSWICK MILITARY HERITAGE PROJECT

The New Brunswick Military Heritage Project, a non-profit organization devoted to public awareness of the remarkable military heritage of the province, is an initiative of the Military and Strategic Studies Program of the University of New Brunswick. The organization consists of museum professionals, teachers, university professors, graduate students, active and retired members of the Canadian armed forces, and other historians. We welcome public involvement. People who have ideas for books or information for our database can contact us through our Web site: www.unb.ca/nbmhp.

One of the main activities of the New Brunswick Military Heritage Project is the publication of the New Brunswick Military Heritage Series with Goose Lane Editions. This series of books is under the direction of Marc Milner, Director of the Military and Strategic Studies Program, and J. Brent Wilson, Research Director of the Centre for Conflict Sudies, both at the University of New Brunswick. Publication of the series is supported by a grant from the Canadian War Musuem.

ABOUT THE AUTHOR

Major Chris M. Hand, Royal Canadian Regiment, is on active duty with the Canadian Armed Forces. He has served on a number of overseas postings, including Bosnia, where he was an infantry company commander, and Warminster, England, where he was under secondment to the British Army. *The Siege of Fort Beausejour, 1755*, is based on his University of New Brunswick master's thesis in history, which he completed in 2002 while serving at Canadian Forces Base Gagetown.